LB
3044
.A35

The administration of
learning resources centers.

THE ADMINISTRATION OF LEARNING RESOURCES CENTERS

with an introductory chapter by

Bob W. Miller, Ed.D.
Director, Community College Programs
North Texas State University

Jack D. Terry, Jr., Ed.D.
Robert W. Hotes, M.A.
Editors

University Press of America

Copyright © 1978 by

University Press of America™
division of
R.F. Publishing, Inc.
4710 Auth Place, S.E., Washington, D.C. 20023

All rights reserved

Printed in the United States of America

ISBN # 0-8191-0274-1

ACKNOWLEDGMENTS

Any volume like an edition on The Administration of Learning Resources Centers owes a lot of thanks to a lot of people who helped make the volume possible. We owe special thanks to those who contributed articles to the volume--without them, the book simply would not exist.

Many people at North Texas State University and Southwestern Baptist Theological Seminary have given us invaluable help in the form of comments, criticisms, and suggestions. Much of the initial development and organization of this volume was prompted by Bob W. Miller who made the task much easier. Dorothy Pulley has given us assistance far above and beyond the call of duty. Editorial assistance was given by Aubrey Sharpe for which we are most grateful. Mrs. Bob Hotes provided diagrams and etchings for the text which lends life to the printed page.

Most of all, our thanks to our families who patiently endured the production of this volume and the many hours of painstaking editing for final publishing. Without their support the task would have been a drudgery rather than a pleasure.

Jack D. Terry, Jr.

Bob Hotes

TABLE OF CONTENTS

ACKNOWLEDGMENTS   ii

INTRODUCTION by Bob W. Miller   1

Chapter I
    I. CONCEPTUAL ADMINISTRATIVE PRINCIPLES
        IN THE MANAGEMENT OF LEARNING RE-
        SOURCES CENTERS by Jack D. Terry, Jr. . . .   9

   II. ADMINISTRATIVE LEADERSHIP AND MANAGE-
       MENT MODELS FOR LEARNING RESOURCES
       CENTERS by Mostafa Hedayatnia   29

  III. THE LEARNING RESOURCE CENTER MANAGER
       AS AN EDUCATOR by Delois Smith   46

  IV. ROLE AND RESPONSIBILITIES OF LEARNING
       RESOURCE CENTER MANAGERS by Larry
       Hunt   62

   V. COMMUNICATION: A CRITICAL FUNCTION IN
       LEARNING RESOURCE CENTER MANAGE-
       MENT by Bob Hotes   74

  VI. LEARNING RESOURCES AND INSTRUCTIONAL
       DEVELOPMENT by Aylene Hegar   98

 VII. SERVICES AND MATERIALS PROVIDED
       THROUGH A LEARNING RESOURCE CENTER
       by Kenneth Roach 108

VIII. ESSENTIALS FOR AN EFFECTIVE LEARNING
       ENVIRONMENT by Aubrey D. Sharpe 128

APPENDIX 140

INTRODUCTION

Bob W. Miller, Ed. D.

This book has been written as a combined effort of members of a doctoral class in "The Administration of Learning Resources." The book emphasizes administration and leadership components more than audiovisual hardward and software or library services.

In preparing the chapters of this book, the basic assumption has been made that learning resource administrators are well prepared through basic curricula in the learning resources areas of audiovisual and library materials but may have had in their studies little emphasis on management theories and techniques.

The learning resources administrator, whether a dean, associate dean, director, or administrator with some other title, is in a line position when dealing with his own staff, but is usually in a staff relationship when dealing with other administrators and faculty members. In this latter position, the title and position of the administrator is valuable only in so far as the individual is able to influence people not under his or her direct supervision.

The learning resources chief administrator usually reports directly to the Dean of Instruction, the Dean of Student Development, an Academic Vice President or the President of the college or campus. It is the perception of the members of this class and several authorities in the field that the chief learning resources administrator should report to the Dean of Instruction or the Vice President of Instruction in order that all instructional functions may be coordinated by one leadership area. The principle that the learning resources operation is a service component for students, faculty and administration, designed to aid in the improvement of the educational program, should be kept in mind.

In later chapters of this book topics such as management by objectives, leadership, motivation, communication and other important items in administration and management will be discussed in detail.

In the administration of learning resources it is important for all staff members to be aware of organizational goals for the entire college or college district. In addition, those who work in the learning resources area should be cognizant of campus goals. Specific objectives should then be written in operational terms for the learning resources centers. These specific objectives must coincide with the district's organizational goals.

In directing the activities of the learning resources center it is necessary that "top management" in the college be sold on the benefits of a learning resources center. To be effective, planning, implementing and evaluating must occur in coordination with superordinates in the organization as well as with subordinates.

The LRE administration must constantly be aware of three basic functions, all three of which must maintain quality control factors:

(1) Maintenance--Many fine operations have gone on in the past in most learning resource centers. These excellent services should not be abandoned. They can be carried into further operation as they presently exist. There is no need to "reinvent the wheel" when an operation is sound.

(2) Problem solving--One of the functions of any administrator is to define and solve problems or make decisions which will affect the entire organizational structure. There is no question that it takes courage to solve problems or to make decisions.

(3) Innovative procedures--Any organization will die if it does not make progress. In other words, an organization cannot remain at "status quo"; it moves forward or regresses. New ideas, modifications of existing procedures will cause an organization to move "Up and beyond" traditional operation.

Success for the Organization

Any educational operation's number one goal is to get effective and efficient results in production, improvement of instruction, providing op portunities for students to get the best education possible, or similar kinds of activities. In an educational institution the priority goal is the best possible education for students. To achieve results, organizational goals must be set for the entire institution and made available to all employees.

The individual employees' goals and objectives are also important. The happier an individual is with his work, the better the morale and esprit de corps in the organization, usually resulting in better performance by each employee.

Both the organization and the employee will have difficulties in doing the job effectively unless short and long range planning occurs. Some cities have already planned to the year 2000. It has been said that business and industry will find it difficult if they have not planned at least ten years in advance. Education will face similar circumstances unless short and long range planning is accomplished specifically within an organization.

Communication plays an important role in an organization with relation to the following questions: Have goals and objectives been developed? Have goals and objectives been communicated? Have goals and objectives been agreed upon? Has there been coordinated planning?

Administrators should consider criteria for objectives in the organization as follows:

(1) Are the objectives complete?
(2) Are the objectives specific?
(3) Do the objectives obtain end results?
(4) Are the objectives measurable?
(5) Are the objectives obtainable with "stretch"?
(6) Do the short and long range objectives correlate with each other?

When talking with employees about objectives and institutional goals, make sure that the scope has not been defined too narrowly. If we have decided upon written goals and objectives for the future, it makes day-to-day decisions easier, because we know what we want to do and where we want to go.

Management Necessities

Any manager or administrator to be effective and efficient must include in his mode of operation the following items:
1. Detailed planning
2. Quality control considerations
3. Accountability or responsibility factors

4. The concept of managing for results
5. Mission, goal and objective statements
6. Wide open operation: "We can't keep subordinates in the dark"
7. Involvement and participation of all employees in the organization

If the preceding items are not taken into consideration, we will probably operate on "management by crisis."

Effective and efficient management is hard work when management, planning, implementation, and evaluation takes place. It should not become just a "paper process" but one which is aimed at obtaining action and results.

There needs to be a process in any organization whereby superordinates and subordinates define responsibility in terms of results, jointly identifying commonalities which can be utilized as guides to operate and to assess contributions.

The individual within the organization should be assisted in setting personal objectives. Steps which could be effective are as follows:

1. Set specific objectives (which could include behavioral objectives and anticipated outcomes).
2. Environmental analysis (is the objective feasible--is the time, staff, hardware, software and other resources available to accomplish the job?)
3. A plan or alternative plans for action (how exactly do you hope to accomplish your objective?)
4. Deadlines, timetables or PERT charts for objectives to be accomplished.
5. Evaluation of the objective. This is an accountability factor, a plan of action, for the individual educator's personal plan of action for successful results.

These specific plans should be in writing and approved by the immediate supervisor.

It is most difficult for an employee to be responsible for an objective that he or she has not accepted on a personal basis. The ultimate question is "Who is setting the goals for whom?"

When writing objectives an excellent technique to utilize is:
To (action verb) (end result) (subject) (time element). Example:
To sell $500,000 of Product Z by January 1st, 19__.

The Leadership Domain

It is important for administrators to develop specific leadership capacities if they are to influence people within the organization.

We should constantly keep in mind that leadership renders a service; leadership is the ability to make decisions; leadership is a willingness to be different when necessary.

A leader must realize that there are specific conditions under which potential is realized in people.

1. An adequate sense of security is necessary in relation to an employee's superordinate
2. The employee should have the opportunity to participate in solution of problems that may affect him.
3. The employee should have the opportunity to assume responsibility as he becomes ready for it.
4. The employee should have the right to appeal "over the head" of his immediate supervisor. (This does not mean the right to " cut the throat of his immediate supervisor.") [1]

The LRC administrator must have "peripheral vision and knowledge" instead of "tunnel vision and knowledge" to be effective and efficient. For example, this individual will have to know about team teaching, systems approach to instruction, acyclic (rapid change) programs, contingency management, autotutorial approaches, management by objectives, continuous progress education, competency based instruction as well as other strategies in the instructional domain. Without this type of knowledge it is doubtful that he or she will be of real service to faculty and students.

Problems Will Arise If You Do Anything

In the past it has been said that it takes a concept in education seventy-five years to cross the United States. One of the evident reasons for this problem is that educators are basically opposed to change. When you are a leader and you step out of the traditional mold, you can expect some problems with people.

Some Problems--We Know!

Business managers.--They may not see the need to spend money in certain areas. Because of financial aspects, they begin to start making instructional decisions instead of business decisions.

Parents.--In the case of modern math (which is no longer modern), for example, parents may object to their offspring being used as guinea pigs. They do not understand this kind of learning process, especially when taught by a strategy such as educational packaging.

Superordinates.--You may become a threat to your boss. He or she may be afraid to support you because you may eventually take over his position.

Subordinates.--Staff and faculty members may have to do more work because of your dynamic leadership. They may have to change lesson plans, syllabi, or even methods and strategies of teaching. There is also more work placed on faculty members because of upgrading, retreading, and retraining processes.

Planning experts and architects.--Example: they may not be able to design a round building, a flexible building; they may not be able to understand the concept of carpet with multiple plug-ins in the floor. Basically, they are not educational architects and do not understand educational programming.

Colleagues on other campuses.--Jealousies may exist because of your progress and action results. These people do not have a positive, pragmatic attitude; therefore they attempt to "shoot down" your program.

Some Solutions--We Hope!

Administrators should have the ability to delegate, trust, and hold others accountable. One cannot do all jobs in the organization. It is important that a leader delegate at the top to release leadership in the ranks. We need to consistently make experts out of subordinates and colleagues.

Modeling. --Much can be learned by studying different models of administration. Often pilot projects could be utilized in one area of the campus to determine if a plan will work before committing total instructional resources for an entire campus.

Avoid defensive mechanisms. --We must go the positive route instead of becoming negative or defensive when an idea is thrown out for consideration by others. Administrators usually lose respect and prestige when they become defensive with others.

Management by objectives. --This is an excellent problem solving, creative or innovative, decision making, and maintenance technique to get the job done through people. It is one of the most efficient ways of getting input from faculty.

Consultants--These educators who really know their business can come from the outside, give fresh ideas, evaluations and analyses to an organization. They can influence employees about more effective and efficient ways of getting things done.

"Ad hoc task forces."--Instead of committees, task forces may be formulated to combine together to accomplish a common goal or objective. Once these task forces have done their job, they should be released to do another job.

Some Questions--to Ask!

1. Can I get the job done without gambling? What are the probabilities that I will always have the information I need, or do I gamble in some situations to play hunches?

2. Is the battle worth winning or losing?

3. Should I be totally honest, laying all cards on the table (no under-the-table dealings)?

4. How do we communicate plans, objectives and expected outcomes (to subordinates, students and parents)?

5. Is the faculty and staff "READY" for this project? When do you pull back or pull off of a project if you find them not ready?

6. When will the perfect time for this change be? Or will there ever be the perfect time?

7. How can I influence others; or how do I "engineer their consent?"

8. When can I be the "good guy," and when do I have to be the guy who wears the "black hat?"

9. How do I leave people with human worth and dignity when I do have to wear the "black hat?"

10. How do I (we) get rid of double standards; one for management and one for workers?

11. How do we get employees to contribute new ideas, to be creative, to sell their ideas?

12. How do you get educators to "stop talking a good game" and to bring about real action?

The remainder of the book will deal with specifics and generalities which should assist the LRC administrator in his everyday operations.

CHAPTER BIBLIOGRAPHY

[1] McGregor, Douglas, Leadership and Motivation, Cambridge, Mass., the M.I.T. Press, 1966.

CHAPTER I

CONCEPTUAL ADMINISTRATIVE PRINCIPLES IN THE MANAGEMENT OF LEARNING RESOURCE CENTERS

Jack D. Terry, Jr.

The concept of administration as it relates to management appears to be caught in a web of transitional trauma, especially in its relationship to academic institutions. Accepted patterns and programs of administration are being thoroughly examined in a search for validity and acceptability of process. Innovative processes of management by performance, management by participation, and management by objectives are being forged into rigid, traditional stoic patterns of academic administration.

The same kinds of managerial concepts are being studied and applied in the management of Learning Resources Centers. Many traditional university libraries are being challenged concerning provisions for readiness in learning and are having to rethink the accepted concepts of print vs. non-print materials. Out of these studies models and designs are beginning to develop which provide guidelines for the implementation of managerial processes in the evolving conceptual thinking of libraries as Learning Resource Centers. A study reported in Audiovisual Instruction (November 1974), "A competency and Task List for Specialists and Technicians in Media Management, Media Product Development, and Instructional Program Development," indicates a trend toward a more sophisticated process of administration which is more management centered and competency oriented.

Peter Drucker, who introduced the concept of management by objectives in 1954 (12, p. 4), later developed a model of new realities in administration and management which sets the tone for this study of conceptual administrative principles of management. Drucker's assumptions related to management realities of our time:

1. Every major task of developed society is being carried out in and through an organized and managed institution.

2. Because our society is rapidly becoming a society of organizations, all institutions, including business, will have to hold themselves accountable for the 'quality of life.'
3. Entrepreneurial innovation will be as important to management as the managerial function.
4. A primary task of management will increasingly be to make knowledge productive.
5. There are management tools and techniques. There are management concepts and principles. There is a common language of management. And there may be a universal 'discipline' of management.
6. Management creates economic and social development. Development is the results of management. (6, pp. 32-40)

Using these assumptions as guidelines, this chapter will explore two competencies necessary for effective management: first, the management planning process and the patterns of management involved in an effective organization. These competencies will be directly related to the management of Learning Resources Centers list of competencies (15, January 26, 1976).

Management Planning Process

Although there are many facets of the management planning process, the following major segments will be considered: (1) the establishment and continuance of a dynamic organization; (2) the human side of management; (3) the process of continued motivational techniques; and, (4) the competency to assist the instructional process through management. Each of these is critically necessary for effective management of a Learning Resources Center.

Dynamic Organization

What constitutes a dynamic, aggressive organization? What are the factors that differentiate the growing prospering organization from the organization of "status quo?" The answer is simple in statement but difficult in implementation. Those who lead and manage teach themselves to change. A dynamic organization is developed and continued on planned change. Blake and Mouton in Building a Dynamic Corporation Through Grid Organization Development establish a seven step model to organizational development. These principles, if put into practice, could become the main-line strategy for the management of Learning Resources Centers. The principles are:

1. To change a company, it is necessary to change the whole company.
2. To change a company, it is necessary for those who head the company to lead the change of it.
3. To change a company, the effort must be a do-it-yourself, a pick-yourself-up-by-the-bootstraps operation.
4. To change a company, it is necessary to apply systematic ways of thinking and analysis to achieve a corporate model of excellence.
5. To change a company it is necessary to see, understand and get people committed to changing all of those activities which are at present not what they should be.
6. To change a company, it is necessary for those leading and managing to study their own company situation in specific, operational terms.
7. To change a company, it is necessary to proceed in a sequential and orderly way. (3, pp. 10-15)

These principles would certainly set a managerial process on a path toward a growing dynamic organization. The change principle appears to be a growing concern of all areas of academic life and the Learning Resources Center is not exempt.

It is clear that universities and colleges are under strong pressure to change, and that such pressure is unlikely to go away in the future. Academic institutions, whether they like it or not, are becoming increasingly open systems as they function in increasingly turbulent, changing competitive environments. If and when good systems change, some members within the academic system will gain or lose power. Some will go down fighting; others may try to figure out how to shift directions and join new movements. (19, pp. 289-90)

The change principle must be carefully considered in the management planning process if a dynamic organization is to evolve.

The Human Side of Management

However, in the midst of dynamic change critical notice

must be taken of the working force within that dynamic. Management processes have a tendency to de-humanize the working man for the elevation of the organization. This principle is, just as the principle of resisting change, destructive to a dynamic organization. Constant notice must be taken of the individual in the organization, recognizing first that he is a person of worth and secondly that he functions as a member of a dynamic group. The planning process of the organization is of vital interest to the person and the group. How can a dynamic organization such as a Learning Resources Center insure the humanizing of its workers? Perhaps the answer lies in the process called Management by Objectives. As John W. Humble notes:

> Management by objectives differs only in that it permits the man himself to determine his own bait from a limited range of choice. Having done so, the MBO process assumes that he will (a) work hard to get it, (b) be pushed internally by reason of his commitment, and (c) make himself responsible to his organization for doing so. (12, p. 5)

The human side of management attempts to encourage the subordinate to excellence, for, in the words of David W. Ewing:

> ... when a plan affects his area of work, the first thing he wants to know is how it affects him. What bearing will it have on his desire for recognition, security, advancement, interesting work? If change in his behavior is called for, will he be able to do it himself or will he have to be changed by someone else? Under the plan, can he remain true to his ideas about what is appropriate and fitting for him to do? (7, pp. 59-60)

Managers of Learning Resources Centers are exploring various models of management by participation in order to develop a Learning Resource team committed to excellence in management, development, and production of instructional media. Several line and staff models of organizational structure have given way to a more team-oriented structure which allows all participants the opportunity of input into the organization (see fig. 1). Attempts to make the weakest member of the organization as responsible as the chief administrator are being developed in many resource centers. Note the model of a Learning Resources Center (This model was developed by Dick Smith, Assistant Dean of

Instructional Services, Richland College, a campus of the Dallas County Community Colleges, for the purpose of demonstrating a participative flow sequence) which is a participative flow diagram. The concept involved in this model is to illustrate an equal responsibility of all persons involved in the Learning Resources Center based upon personal goals and objectives set by each person in the organization. Each level of responsibility is relational and depends upon other participants in the organization for completeness. This process model identifies the humanizing effect of Management by Objectives as expressed in the following task analysis model:

(1) The man clarifies his tasks and commits himself to new challenges of a meaningful kind.
(2) He participates with his boss in doing this.
(3) He works with his colleagues in teams and task forces where a common problem is to be solved.
(4) These task forces help to acquire skills of working effectively as a group by practical methods that don't expose all their personal fears and motives.
(5) They build on the strengths and weaknesses of colleagues. (12, p. 11)

Continued Motivation Techniques

What is the best means of providing incentive motivation to all levels of a Learning Resources Center organizations? What is motivation and what techniques can be employed to produce more efficient service and better commitment? A classic definition of motivation is:

. . . to steer one's actions toward certain goals and to commit a certain part of one's emergies to reaching them. Each person's pattern of steering and committing is usually learned over a lifetime; it represents his way of trying to come to satisfactory terms with his environment. (9, p. 34)

However, this discussion goes beyond the classic term motivation and explores the concept of continued motivation. Continued motivation is the stake that a person has in his responsibility regardless of the level of participation which makes his task in the organization worth getting up for each day. It is the excitement of the possibilities of the day in line with the stated

LEARNING RESOURCE MANAGEMENT FLOW DESIGN

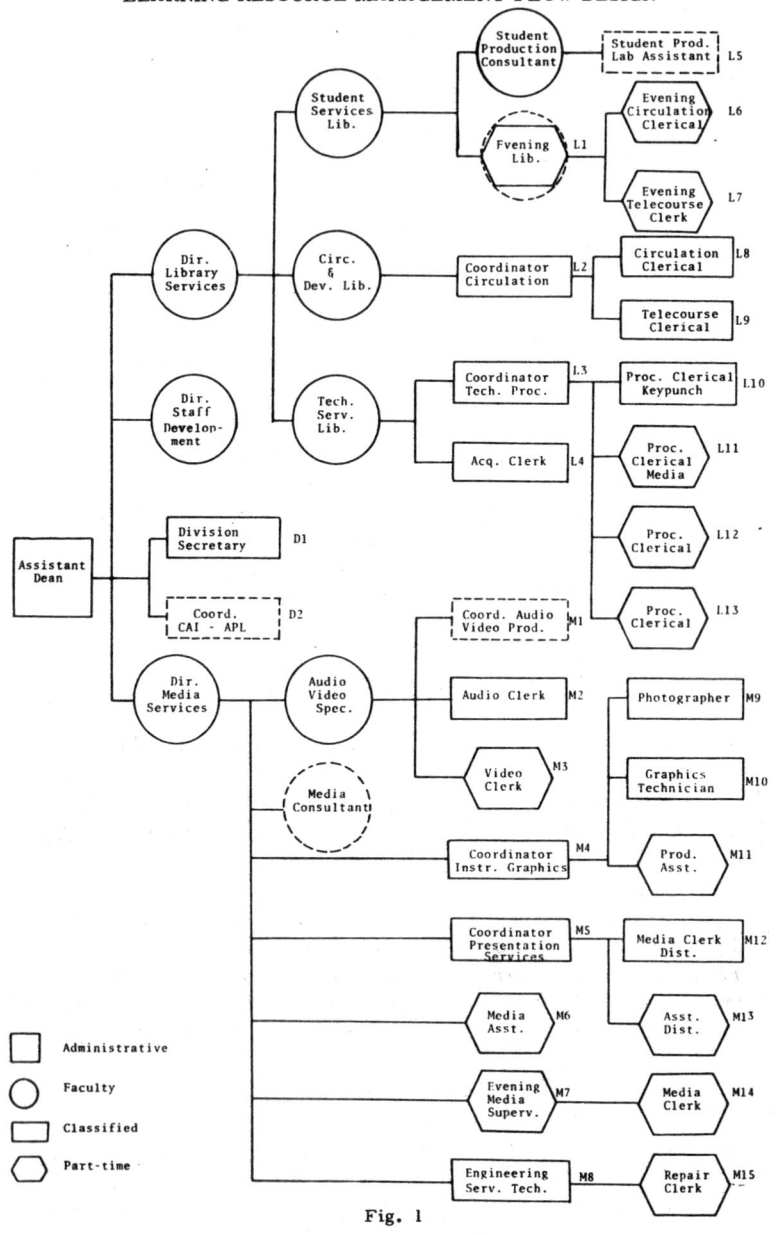

Fig. 1

personal goals and objectives to be achieved for the more effective operation of that part of the Learning Resource Center which is personally claimed as a responsibility.

Motivation and a continuing excitement of motivation is a built-in process of Management by Objectives. The nature of the plan of MBO provides the person an opportunity to look expectantly to each day of work with achievement in mind. The three parts of MBO which speak to continued motivation are: (1) involvement, (2) participation, and (3) autonomy.

> (1) Involvement.--Involvement in this sense requires mutually negotiated involvement of the individual to design his own activities. It is generally agreed that the incumbent probably has a greater awareness, a deeper sensitivity, and a clearer understanding of the problems involved. He can develop a sense of entrepreneurship about his job, or stated another way he begins to take ownership of the responsibility for accomplishing the job.
> (2) Participation.--Participation is the opportunity to bring together all the skills an individual possesses and apply these for the total problem-solving process of the enterprise. This allows total participation of all viewpoints which exists.
> (3) Autonomy.--Autonomy is the opportunity to participate and be allowed to manage that part of the task assigned. It also involves the privilege of making mistakes, taking risks, and generally failing or succeeding within the job. (21, pp. 28-29)

As a person is allowed more involvement participation, and autonomy in his responsibilities, the motivation aspect of that responsibility became intensified because the full success or failure is resting on the person's shoulder.

Competency to Assist the Instructional Process

A final consideration in the development of a managerial process for learning resources is the principle of assistance to instructional design. An adequate Learning Resources Center must provide multi-faceted developmental processes to assist the teacher in more effective instruction. Current literature is replete with instructional developmental products. Planning for Higher Education (June 1975) states, "Our job is simply to provide any professor on this campus with the widest range of options for strengthening and enlivening his teaching. The decision whether to use them and how, is his." This statement is expressive of the feeling of Learning Resources Centers on college campuses across the country. Products provisions and multi-mediated assistance appears to be the prime reason of existence.

Keegan (13, p. 35), Patterson (17, p. 59), Vitrogam (22, p. 44), (10, p. 26) and Neuhauser (16, p. 36) all express the determined reason for existence of a Learning Resources Center, namely instructional assistance. Gorman (10) established this model as the initial instructional management function of a resource center. His claim is that an efficient operation will be capable of preparing for and equipping teachers to perform the kind of instruction identified in the model (see fig. 2).

Faseler and West (8, p. 43), Tiagarajan (20, p. 38) and Macey (14, p. 42) identify the proper administration and management of learning resource centers as the means of improved evaluation and development of instructional program integration. Faseler and West conclude in an article in Educational Technology which sums up the necessity of competency in assisting the instructional process as follows:

> One of the greatest challenges facing the media administrator is to derive the most educational benefits from the schools' media investment. This necessitates extensive planning and careful management. (8, p. 45)

The management planning process includes four important criterion which must be taken into consideration by the Learning Resources Manager. These are:

(1) The establishment of a dynamic organization.
(2) The appropriate understanding of the human side of management.
(3) A managerial process which promotes and provides for continued motivation.
(4) An indepth understanding of the process involved in an adequate program of instructional design development.

INSTRUCTIONAL MANAGEMENT FUNCTIONS

Communication	Physical Support	Monitoring
1. Provides an array of tasks	1. Reflects the nature of learning	1. Maintains facility and materials
2. Defines task clearly	2. Organized into a learning station	2. Monitors materials
3. Provides levels of performance	3. Supports the task	3. Provides for learner assistance
4. Rationals provided	4. Prerequisite needs identified	4. Receives learner feedback
5. Prerequisites identified	5. Items used identified	5. Provides confirmation of success and certification
6. Exit, diagnostic, prescription, capability	6. Performance models displayed	
7. Task organized	7. Staff both visible and accessible	
8. Presentation controlled by learner	8. Open for extended periods to accommodate learner needs	
9. Performance observable		
10. Provides for application		
11. Provides self-check		
12. Retention provision		

(10, p. 26)

Fig. 2

Patterns for Competent Management

Since Management by Objectives has already been mentioned in this chapter, an expansion of that concept is necessary to completely understand the pattern of management suggested for learning resource centers. There is an almost endless list of authors and writers who have contributed to the MBO literature which is sometimes referred to as management by results, management by participation, planning and organizing for results or standards of performance, goal setting, expected results, measurements, planning and reviewing performance, planning and reviewing, performance standards or old management (21, pp. 3, 4). No matter what process or nomenclature is used, the concept of the process is deciding where the desired result lies (the individual's objective and the organizational goal) and then finding the most acceptable process for both superordinate and subordinate for reaching that goal. The model (fig. 3) expresses this concept. How can this pattern of management become a useful plan of action for learning resource centers?

Formal Plan of Action

Management by Objectives can become the formal plan of action for a LRC. This concept is a dynamic system which seeks to integrate needs, clarify goals, and contribute to the development of self actualization. When a worthwhile system of management by objectives is in operation, there is a continuous process of:

1. Reviewing critically and restating strategies and tactical plans.
2. Clarifying by results and performance standards in line with unit and total goals and the contribution and commitment to these individually and as a team member.
3. Agreeing on a job improvement plan which makes measurable and realistic contribution to the unit and total goal for better performance.
4. Providing conditions in which it is possible to achieve key results and carry out the improvement plan, notably an organization structure which gives a manager maximum freedom and flexibility in operation, and management control information in a form and at a frequency which make for more effective self-control and better and quicker decisions.

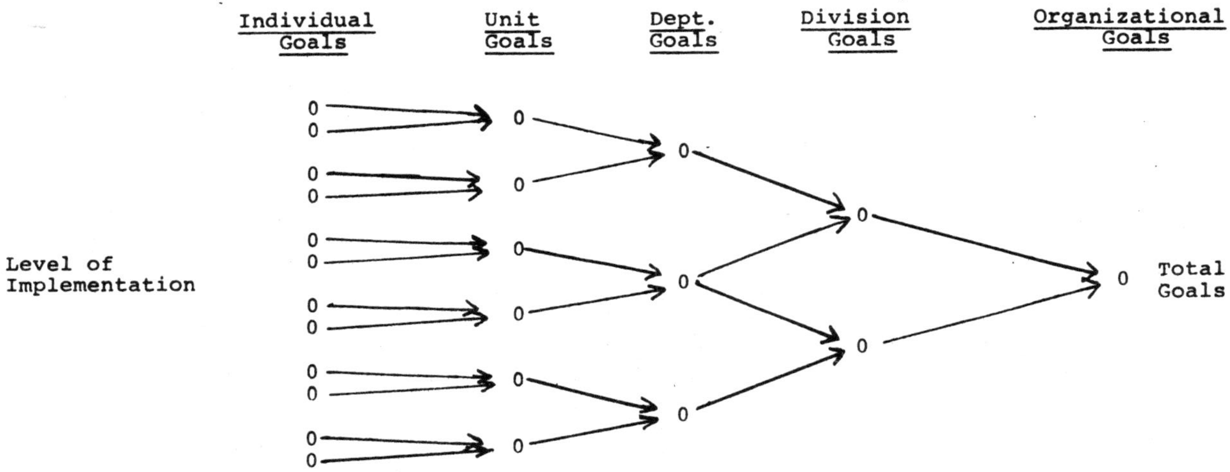
Individual Goals
Unit Goals
Dept. Goals
Division Goals
Organizational Goals
Level of Implementation
Total Goals

(22, p. 4)

Fig. 3

5. Using a systematic performance reivew to measure progress toward results and potential review to identify men with potential for advancement.
6. Developing management training plans to help each manager to overcome his weakness, build on his strengths, and accept responsibility for self-development.
7. Strengthen a manager's motivation by effective selection, salary and succession plans. (12, pp. 33, 34)

This formal plan of action appears in the model (fig. 4).

Clarification of Organizational Design

In any organization, and especially in a learning resource center using management by objectives as a formal plan of action, there needs to be a clarification of the organization design; that is, a clear understanding how the process is going to work at each level of operation from top management down to custodial service. The organizational design for getting the job done is simple in construct but sometime tough to place in operation. It follows a sequence which all people in the organization whether chief administrators, mid-managers or unit directors need to clearly understand.

The first management function is planning which involves deciding where you want to go and what the basic goals and plans for accomplishing the work will be. The second function is organizing, which is deciding how you are going to marshal the human, physical and other resources necessary to accomplish the task. Third is the actual performing of the responsibilities. Fourth is controlling or making sure that the responsibilities are carried out in accordance with the plan set forth in the first place. Fifth is the measuring function, which is the final step in the management process and involves looking over the work that has been done and determining whether it meets the basic objectives, standards and criteria set out in the original plan. (21, p. 55).

A conceptual design of this organizational clarification might look like this (fig. 5).

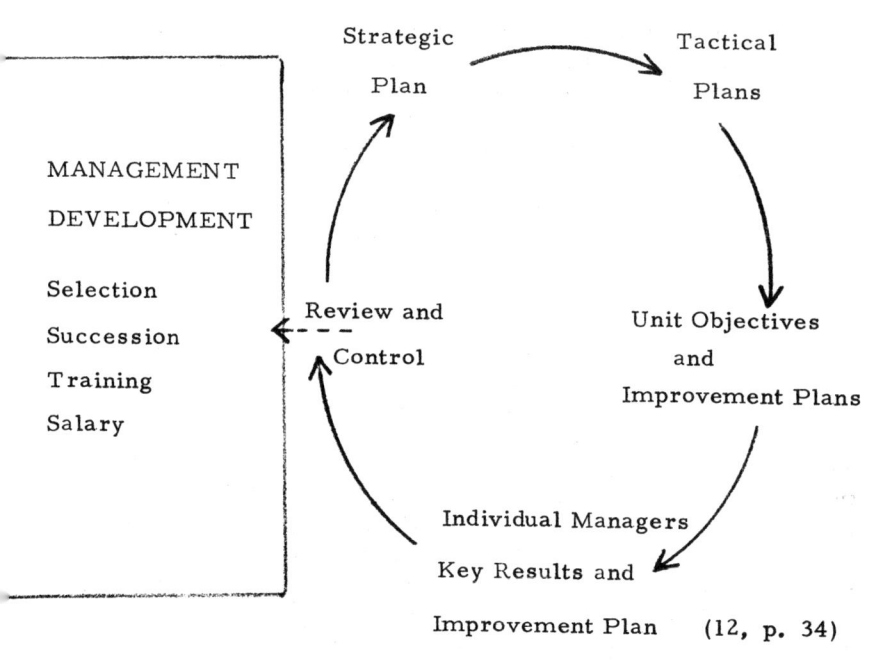

```
                        Strategic          Tactical
                          Plan              Plans

MANAGEMENT
DEVELOPMENT

Selection
Succession      Review and              Unit Objectives
Training         Control                      and
Salary                                  Improvement Plans


                       Individual Managers
                       Key Results and
                       Improvement Plan        (12, p. 34)
```

Fig. 4

Reprinted by permission of the publisher from HOW TO MANAGE BY OBJECTIVES, John W. Humble c 1973 by John W. Humble. Published by AMACOM, a division of American Management Associations.

```
                            Goals - How to
Planning ————————— Get it done

Organization ——————— Who will do it:

Performing ———————— Doing the work

                            Making sure it's
Controlling ——————— done right

Reviewing —————————— Summarizing results
```

Fig. 5

For reference to an organizational chart, look back to the first part of this chapter and review the organizational diagram presented from Richland College in Dallas, Texas (fig. 1).

Performance Standards

Recall from the last section that item three of the organizational design in figure 5 had to do with performing. In learning resource centers the performing criteria will vary from position to position and from job description to job description. Since this is true of all job responsibilities, somewhere there must be some standard of criteria for a specialist in media management. Audio-visual Instruction, November 1974, provided just such a list. A composite list of competencies for media management would contain the following responsibilities.

I. Organizational Management Function
    1. To set goals/policy of the training center.
    2. To organize and reorganize organizational structure to meet goals.
    3. To plan operations for the coming year.
    4. To coordinate facilities planning.
    5. To plan programs/projects.
    6. To initiate agency-funded projects.
    7. To formulate policy for procedure and equipment changes in the center.
    8. To monitor and change operation of the center.
    9. To improve communications in the center.
    10. To administer the training center.
    11. To administer and direct projects.
    12. To administer training courses.
    13. To develop a model for economic analysis of training.
    14. To design the financial structure.
    15. To estimate media center budget.
    16. To prepare annual budget report.
    17. To supervise cooperative purchasing.
    18. To purchase audio-visual materials.

II. Personnel Management Function
    1. To staff projects.
    2. To staff training center.
    3. To conduct training of new staff on general office procedures.

4. To set up on-th-job seminars.
5. To improve communications between technicians and artists.
6. To supervise personnel in the training center.
7. To supervise the graphics unit.
8. To supervise graphics unit.
9. To fire personnel.

III. Research-Theory Functions
1. To conceptualize theoretical models.
2. To conduct research projects.
3. To analyze research data.
4. To improve standards of research projects.
5. To perform feasibility study on new equipment.
6. To conduct survey on media usage.

IV. Design Function
1. To design equipment systems.
2. To design improved training equipment.
3. To design new facilities.
4. To plan instructional space.

V. Productive Function
1. To produce audio-visual bulletin.

VI. Evaluation and Selection Function
1. To develop a climate supportive of evaluation.
2. To plan and focus project evaluation.
3. To develop evaluation models and techniques.
4. To collect, process, analyze, and interpret evaluation data.
5. To review and select instructional materials.
6. To evaluate instructional materials.
7. To evaluate film holdings.

VII. Support-Supply Function
1. To improve equipment acquisition procedures.
2. To improve cataloging procedures.
3. To catalog materials.
4. To improve distribution system.
5. To locate curriculum materials.

VIII. Utilization Function
1. To help student identify learning interests and select areas.
2. To help students select learning activities to meet objectives.
3. To lecture or make media presentations to large student groups.
4. To monitor individualized and self instructional media.

IX. Utilization-Dissemination Function
1. To maintain professional status and keep up in the field.
2. To develop dissemination strategies for teacher training project.
3. To explain individualized instruction project to visitors.
4. To provide information on audio-visual centers.
5. To consult on media use and design.
6. To promote increased use of instructional television (ITV).
7. To report to management.
8. To inform teachers on media.
9. To advise product planners on educational market.
10. To facilitate use of company products.
11. To teach basic audio-visual course. (1, pp. 29-39)

For a more complete indepth particulars study of the performance standards of the learning resource center manager, please read Audio-visual Instruction, November 1974.

Analysis and Review of Progress

Suppose a person has agreed on all nine performance standards mentioned in the preceding section, how would that person be evaluated by his superordinate and how in turn would that learning resource center manager evaluate his subordinate? Management by Objectives suggests the establishment of a performance-improvement cycle. A simple list identifies the four main elements of a performance cycle.

1. Define the job.
2. Design expected results
3. Job performance.
4. Measure results.

Numbers one through three were clearly covered in the minute description of management responsibilities. What about number four, measure results? How does the manager perform this task? Peter Drucker states, "For full effectiveness all work needs to be integrated into a unified program for performance (5, p. 195).

There is an excellent criteria established by Varney for analysis and measurement of performance. This criteria could certainly be used to good advantage in a learning resource center. The criteria are:

1. Can the individual responsible for the job control all aspects of the job which affect the expected result, and does the expected result measure a major segment of the individual's responsibility?
2. Can the individual reach the objectives, and will he have to stretch to do so? The objective must not be set so high that it is unattainable.
3. Does the expected result key in directly to the expected results for the individual's boss, for the department, and the company as a whole?
4. Can the expected result be exceeded, and can the individual fall below if he fails to perform on the job? An individual should be able to excel on the job.
5. Is there a way of providing direct feedback to the individual relative to how he is progressing towards the expected result?
6. Can the expected result be clearly measured at the end of the performance time cycle. (21, pp. 92-94)

With these criteria in mind there follows a three-step process for reviewing progress.

(1) Meet with the employee face to face and decide where he he is performing. This involves looking at targets and comparing them to actual performance.

(2) From the meeting diagnose and evaluate the reasons for the existence of the variations above and below the actual targets previously set. Look to the expected results and see if there are any keys why the person performed below or above the particular target.

(3) Design further plans on the diagnosis. This may involve changing the job design or the way the job is structured. In some cases it may mean the establishment of developmental and training programs for the individual to improve the particular areas where help is needed (21, pp. 93-94).

Conclusions

In order to understand more fully conceptual administrative principles in the management of learning resource centers, it was suggested that Management Planning Process contain: (1) a dynamic organization; (2) the humanizing of management so as to make each individual in the organization a being of worth; (3) develop a continuous process of motivation techniques (Management by Objectives was suggested); and, (4) to develop the expertise necessary for the assistance of teachers in the designing of instruction and developing enrichment programs.

As a corollary in patterns of management, it was suggested that learning resource centers consider (1) its formal plan of action as management by objectives which would (2) assist the center in clarifying its organizational design by (3) developing specific performance standards which could be (4) analyzed and measured through a review process for the purpose of assisting the subordinate to enjoy performing the tasks which belong to his job responsibility.

CHAPTER BIBLIOGRAPHY

[1] Audio-visual Instruction, November 1974, Washington, D.C., 1974.

[2] Balderston, E. Frederick, Managing Today's Universities, San Francisco, Jossey-Bass Publishers, 1974.

[3] Blake, Robert R., and Mouton, Jane Srygley, Building a Dynamic Corporation Through Grid Organization Development, Menlo Park, Calif., Addison-Wesley Publishing Co., 1969.

[4] Drucker, Peter F., The Effective Executive, New York, Harper & Row, Publishers, 1967.

[5] Drucker, Peter F., Managing for Results, New York, Harper & Row, 1964.

[6] Drucker, Peter F., Technology, Management and Society, New York, Harper & Row, 1970.

[7] Ewing, David W., The Human Side of Planning, London, Macmillan Co., 1969.

[8] Faseler, Len, and West, Phillip T., "The Media Administrator: Instructional Leader of the Future?" Educational Technology, Vol. 15, No. 7, July 1975.

[9] Gellerman, Saul W., Management by Motivation, American Management Association, Inc., 1968.

[10] Gorman, Don A., "Instructional Management: A Meaningful Alternative," Educational Technology, June 1975.

[11] Gronlund, Norman E., Stating Behavioral Objectives for Classroom Instruction, London, Macmillan Co., 1970.

[12] Humble, John W., How to Manage by Objectives, American Management Association, 1973.

[13] Keegan, John J., "Performance Based Staff Evaluation: A Reality We Must Face," Educational Technology, Vol. 15, No. 11, November 1975.

[14] Macey, Daniel J., "The Role of Process Evaluation in Program Development and Implementation," Educational Technology, Vol. 15, No. 4, April 1975.

[15] Miller, Bob W., Administration of Learning Resources in Higher Education, Class Notes (NTSU EDHE 690), Spring 1976.

[16] Newhauser, Charlotte, "A Management Information System to Facilitate the Functioning of a CBTE Program," Educational Technology, Vol. 15, No. 3, March 1975.

[17] Patterson, Jerry, "Toward Instructional Improvement: A Planning Model for Teacher and Administrators," Educational Technology, Vol. 15, No. 9, September 1975.

[18] Planning for Higher Education, Vol 4, No. 3:4/5, June 1975.

[19] Richman, Barry M., and Farmer, Richard N., Leadership Goals and Power in Higher Education, San Francisco, Jossey-Bass Publishers, 1974.

[20] Thiagarajam, Sivasailam, "Goal-Free Evaluation for Media," Educational Technology, Vol. 15, No. 5, May 1975.

[21] Varney, Glen H., Management by Objectives, Chicago, Dartnell Corp., 1971.

[22] Vitrogan, David, "The Role of the Administrator in the Development of a Self-Paced Personalized System of Instruction," Educational Technology, Vol. 15, No. 8, August 1975.

CHAPTER II

ADMINISTRATIVE LEADERSHIP AND MANAGEMENT MODELS FOR LEARNING RESOURCE CENTERS

Mostafa Hedayatnia

The processes of conceptual management described in the preceding chapter depends upon a comprehensive understanding of administrative styles and competencies. Undoubtedly, every educational institution requires strong and effective leadership, if quality, prestige, and financial strength of that institution are to be preserved.

Several administrative leadership models have been developed for particular situations. They have evolved from bureaucratic model to collegial, and then to political, organized anarchy, and participatory management models. Each model has been conceptualized, defined, and implemented in higher education institutions with controversial results. The answer is that there is no single leadership model for the university or college administrator to rely on for the governance or management of an institution. The executive officer or the top administrator should utilize a variety of approaches to leadership if he is to succeed. This is true as long as the leadership style and model are consistent and that one style is not at the extreme end from the other.

One of the multi-functions of the professional leader-actor is to manage effectively programs for the professional development of his staff. Such programs should be concerned with a joint-venture of the instructional administrator, the learning resources staff members and the teaching faculty in developing their intellectual, affective, and psychomotor skills on the behalf of students.

Developmental growth necessitates meaningful participation of instructional, technical, and other departmental staff in workshops, seminars, conferences, and conventions. Also, other in-service training should include foreign travels, field trips, leave programs, graduate work, and academic exposure, all of which elicit attention to teaching methodology, curriculum development, and utilization of technology.

An administrative innovator should not only participate and persuade his institution's internal constituencies in such developmental endeavors, he will also make sure that necessary human and other resources are being properly allocated. In addition, he will resolve the potential impact of the Learning Resources staff development on the present and future quality of curriculum and instruction.

Educational Leadership

Power and authority are the two fundamental tools of leadership by which the executive officer can keep a university or college running smoothly and in an orderly fashion (10). The term power has been used synonymously with that of authority in the literature or higher education administration. Here authority is defined as institutional power.

In the bureaucratic model of leadership, somewhat between democratic and autocratic models, power exposes itself as hierarchies, predetermined procedures, rules, and regulations (23, p. 29). The long-lived traditional and formal organizational structures are examples of the bureaucratic mode.

The collegial model, on the other hand, places power in the hands of faculty scholars. Here the bureaucratic officials have little influence but the pedagogical team manages its own affairs; and above all, the significance of hierarchy and structure is lost. The main flaw in the bureaucratic model is that the flow of informal information is basically faster than the formal, which seriously damages the social, psychological, and self-actualization needs of the overall constituents of the educational institution. The lack of formal power structure and leadership, however, cannot be counted as a disadvantage to the collegial model.

Another system of governance and leadership is the political model which is an important contribution of the 1970's (23, p. 30). This model takes "conflict as a natural phenomenon" and is mainly concerned with goal-setting at the beginning of the programs. The power in the political model is in the hands of a small group of political elites and interest groups. There is, however, a democratic tendency in colleges and universities toward more participation.

Although the political model has contributed tremendously to the thinking process, understanding, explaining, dealing with conflict, power, and major aspects of decision-making, it can not be adapted to all situations and under all circumstances. A major disadvantage in this model is that it does not deal with the management process; nor does it spell out the duties of the president. This model is essentially descriptive and explanatory.

The latest leadership model, the "organized anarchy model," is practiced in a sample of forty-two colleges and universities around the nation, according to Richman and Farmer (23). In this model, power is somewhat ambiguous, along with the purposes and problematic goals. Also, technology is unclear, participation appears to be shifting, and above all, the top administrator's success becomes entirely unpredictable.

In spite of its ambiguities, the organized anarchy model, based on the "garbage-can" theory, can provide solutions to many financial and other problems confronting university and college administrators. Among the rules and regulations of this model, the advocation of "sensible foolishness" and organizational "playfulness" seems to be prominent. Further, the organized anarchy model can be "a valuable point of departure for developing predictive, prescriptive and operational theories, guidelines, and approaches" (23, p. 33).

Effective leadership is the product of multiple conditions within an organization. To be effective, educational leadership must be consistent with both organizational expectations and beneficial to organizational goals. Further, administrative leadership is identified with goals and objectives, curriculum, instruction, and supervision or coordination. It is evident that leadership remains predominently directed at the individual rather than at the followers or situations in which both operate. Leadership is defined as:

> . . . behavior that causes individuals to move toward goals they find to be important and that creates in the followers a feeling of well being. . . . By assuming the position of supervisor, one indicates willingness to exert leadership and to be held accountable for affecting the behavior of teachers in such a way that the goals of the organization are achieved. Successful instructional supervisory

behavior cannot exist in the absence of effective leadership behavior (9, p. 331).

Perhaps one of the best leadership models which has been conceptualized, structured, and implemented satisfactorily in a higher education institution is the concept of humanistic-governance management (2). This organizational system is concerned with synthesizing and unifying "interpersonal and humanistic actions that should pervade any structural governance management." And administrator, in his multi-function duties such as coordination, direction, decision making, and communication, should be able to integrate systematically with the overall constituencies of the institution for more effective and consistent functioning.

Humanistic governance management emphasizes two categories of leadership. They are: (1) "Establishing and maintaining a positive working climate;" and (2) "Utilizing the team approach in decision making." These two aspects will be discussed below as they are vital to the operational functions of an administrator while interfacing and integrating with the constituents-claimant public.

1. Establishing a positive working climate: an educational administrator can be an effective and efficient leader when he exhibits and develops positive thinking about colleagues in that they progress and benefit from a free and open environment. He also understands and deals with the psychological needs of the faculty by developing an intellectual environment in which every member can contribute and also be rewarded according to his/her capabilities and accomplishments. A mutual respect and understanding between the administrator and colleagues should always be operative.

A common and favorite aspect of the behavioral psychology among the practitioners of higher education is that the administrator has to practice and maintain basic courtesy in dealing with colleagues regardless of the pressures under which he functions and the conflicting demands which are endlessly in operation. In this sequence, the administrator should enhance the dignity of the position he is holding, not at the expense of colleagues but by a "we" attitude toward negotiations and communications, and a team approach toward current problems and issues.

An administrator should function within the limits of the power and the authority which he has been delegated. He therefore has to observe due process in educational affairs, and when action needs to be taken, he should not hesitate. In this process, the administrator should neither play favorites nor respond to noisy complaints and "greasing and squeaky wheels." The former destroys confidence and the latter invites imposition. Instead, he has to carefully adhere to equity in order to build up morale, and respond to complaints by evaluating each situation on its merits and approaching it through an appropriate decision making process.

An administrator, through grievance procedures, should provide for a fair and sincere hearing for the entire academic community. Such human need is expected by the constituencies who often feel they have been the victims of undesirable decisions and wish to be heard sympathetically. The importance of such process is recognized when the administrator believes in and deals with a diverse staff and faculty whose opinions are respected and whose independent thoughts are institutionally supported.

A meaningful working climate requires that the administrative leader allow for a free flow of his co-workers' opinions and ideas in their free and open interpersonal relationship; provided that any unfavorable remakrs, comments, and opinions are not used against them when rewards are distributed. and opinions are not used against them when rewards are distributed. While the educational administrator does not help by developing a personality contest, he should administer a genuine and open system of communication for the betterment of the educational environment. Also, the administrator should evaluate the outcomes of institutional affairs, and see how they will look to and affect his colleagues before he attempts to make a final decision.

2. The team approach: towards a positive "we" attitude and feeling, the educational leader should agree upon and utilize a team approach for planning and problem-solving. While he accepts responsibility in decision making, he should encourage self-initiation and also develop social maturity in his colleagues who may contribute to the concept of the "we" enterprise.

The chief executive, while working with small groups, should believe in and develop a group-centered approach in which all participants have their inputs, share each other's opinions, feelings, and ideas, and make the final decisions, collectively. The administrator should also make certain that such decisions are first reached to those who are affected by the decisions, and if possible, are consulted. The chief administrator is still responsible for the final decision within the organization.

Since the academic community works towards a single goal-- educating the students--all members of the institution should be the first to hear about decisions and important developments. The campus mail and newspapers are two of the best means of information dissemination throughout the campus. Also, each group member should be informed about the processes involved in finalizing a decision and how the solutions and recommendations given by the individual members have been utilized.

From a wide decision making base, originated by group members who are working towards mutually accepted goals, the administrator can witness increasing enthusiasm, and consequently production, which in turn ensures success in the educational enterprise. A wide and effective decision base would materialize by employing input from the top departmental administrators and the faculty members who function in the educational corporation as autonomous "officers" and whose relationships within the institution are neither expected nor labeled as an employer-employee relationship.

As we have seen, the nebulous personalistic function of educational leadership can not be specifically defined in terms of a roadmap to success. However, such a type of leadership, and any other leadership for that matter, draws a tremendous amount of attention from all internal constituencies who are affected by the leadership and from outside forces from whom authority and power have been delegated. A leader has to cope and cooperate with all the parties concerned if his leadership is to be effective and efficient.

One of the aspects of leadership, the reflective, reveals the motives, aspirations, actions, beliefs, and other human traits which constitute the personality of the leader (21, pp. 1-2). Evidently, these idiosyncracies may prove fruitful when they are incorporated with the leader's broad educational background and the demonstration of scholarly views in certain disciplines.

An educational leader may be able to capitalize on his philosophical insights and educational expertise in dealing with the affairs of the institution concerned with the daily problems or issues, and the short and long-range plans.

While the intuitive nature of leadership is quite necessary for handling human relations as well as institutional affairs, the qualitative behavior of the administrator's educational background would prove effective. Additional expertise in respect to industrial management and business would further enhance the leader's capabilities.

The educational administrator should be both an experimenter and an innovator. In the process of decision making, he has to function as a broker in human affairs, for dealing with the heterogeneous character of his clients and their incessant demands, with an impartial attitude. "Engineering of consent" behavior is desirable as far as the administrator's integrity is not affected. An administrator need not be a lawyer, but some knowledge in the law is quite helpful. Furthermore, an administrator has to be able to communicate effectively and enthusiastically, judge people fairly, and be self-motivated, among other things.

Management techniques will surely help an administrator in planning effectively and imaginatively with a vision to the future. Innovation will occur as a result of making sound decisions based on the needs of the institution and the people. Once a leader is able to maintain a friendly atmosphere and aggressive enough to push forward his decisions and also possesses certain refinements in aesthetic appreciation, he will be successful in innovative adventures.

Decision making is perhaps the most important element among the administrator's multi-functions. In such process, a lot of people's demands and aspirations are automatically not accomplished or are completely ignored. A diligent and dependable administrator has to be capable and mature enough to hack the pressure generated from the people's dissatisfactions and discontents. He has to be courageous in handling those affairs.

An effective and efficient leader must develop intuitively the necessary rationale in order to motivate, organize, and control the overall performance of subordinates. As a social man, he has to be responsible for establishing an educational atmosphere in which mutual friendship, care, and understanding are fully developed. Further, a self-actualizing administrator has the potential to delegate authority to his top colleagues in order to develop their talents and participate in the decision making process; and at the same time, he is alert enough to challenge them in critical situations.

From this discussion, it can be inferred that an administrator, in his complex character, should be a broker of human relations. With his intuition and proven expertise, he should be flexible enough to provide leadership to divergent people; while being elusive enough not to let subordinates take advantage of his leadership.

Management of Learning Resources

Administrative leadership in higher education has many functions. A major function is for the top executive to play the role of a change agent in the educational process. To fulfill that requirement, he has to make utilization of available managerial tools. It is also imperative that he, along with other chief administrators, become knowledgeable and participate in Management Information Systems and computers, planning-programming-budgeting systems (PPBS), full-time offices for institutional research, operations research and various kinds of mathematical models, and other modern managerial methods and contemporary innovations that are still much more widespread in business and even in government than in colleges and universities. Higher education's new commitment to systems-oriented budgeting approaches gives a boost to the utilization of managerial techniques (15).

To impose change and also to manage the instructional technology programs, the college chief administrator may find the following guidelines quite helpful:

1. The responsibilities and functions of Learning Resources programs within the instructional structure and the status of the chief administrator and heads of Learning

Resources Units are clearly defined.
2. The relationship of a Learning Resources program to the total educational program necessitates involvement of the professional staff in all areas and levels of academic planning.
3. Advisory committees composed of faculty and students are essential for the evaluation and extension of services.
4. The chief administrator is responsible for the administration of the Learning Resources program, which is carried out by means of established lines of authority, definition of responsibilities, and channels of communication through heads of Learning Resources Units as defined in writing.
5. Internal administration of a Learning Resources program is based on staff participation in policy, procedural, and personal decisions.
6. Budget planning and implementation of Learning Resources program is the responsibility of the chief administrator.
7. The accumulation of pertinent statistics and maintenance of adequate records is a management responsibility.
8. Adequate management includes the preparation and dissemination of information to administration, faculty, and students concerning activities, services, and materials.
9. Responsibilities for all learning resources and services should be assigned to a central administration unit.
10. Multi-campus districts take advantage of the opportunity for close cooperation, exchange of resources, and shared technical processes while providing full resources and services for every campus (1, pp. 54-56).

The guidelines specifically indicate that the chief administrator and the head of learning resources unit work closely with other top administrators of the college, faculty, and professional staff members towards the instructional programs which meet the needs of their clients. Obviously, no one person should be responsible for the total education of an individual or a group of students (22, p. 3; 5, p. 110).

Approaches to instructional programs can not be an adaptation of traditional methods, nor should they be handled single-handedly by the faculty members. Instructional technology as a new paradigm is concerned with "gestalt," an organized configuration for the purpose of sharing experiences, responsibilities, or acts. That is, educational programs should be an integrated complex of media utilization, machinery, methodology, and personnel, including the subject-matter content all structured as a single unit with a schedule of time and sequential phasing. As Robert Heinich puts it:

> Management of learning (or instructional management) includes the interrelationships of not only all instructional events in the instructional process, but also logistical, sociological, and economic factors. The system of instructional management . . . is referred to as 'technology of education,' where technology is defined as a 'complex, integrated organization of men and machines, of ideas, of procedures, and of management.' (13, p. 106)

The traditional audiovisual aids (e.g., slides, film strips, transparencies, etc.) usually entered at the classroom implementation level as the figure 1 indicates. At this level, the teacher is seeking materials that might help him in his instruction. Also, at this point, the audiovisual director instituted a search of catalogs for appropriate materials (13, p. 116).

As the term audiovisual changed to Educational Media, and then to Instructional Technology during the last two decades, so did the newer media (e.g., TV, film courses, language labs, programmed instruction, and sophisticated packages, etc.) enter the instructional process. The newer media, unlike traditional audiovisual materials have entered the instructional process at the curriculum planning level as illustrated in figure 2.

This shift of emphasis from classroom implementation to the curriculum planning level has pushed many professionals in the field toward the utilization of the systems approach in managing the Learning Resources programs and in problem solving. New resources are currently being allocated, and new directions are discovered for proper implementation. For example, at the curriculum planning level (strategy), instruction is dichotomized into the mediated instruction and the classroom instruction as shown in figure 3. The term mediated instruction indicates any

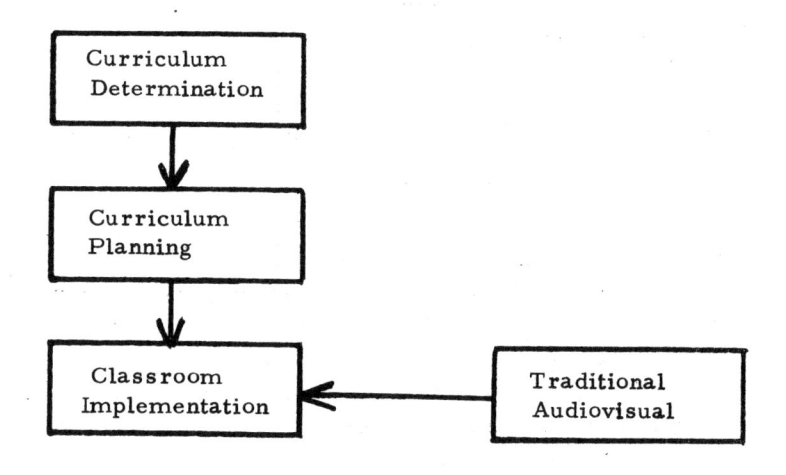

Fig. 1.--The Entry of Traditional Audiovisual Aids into the Instructional Process.

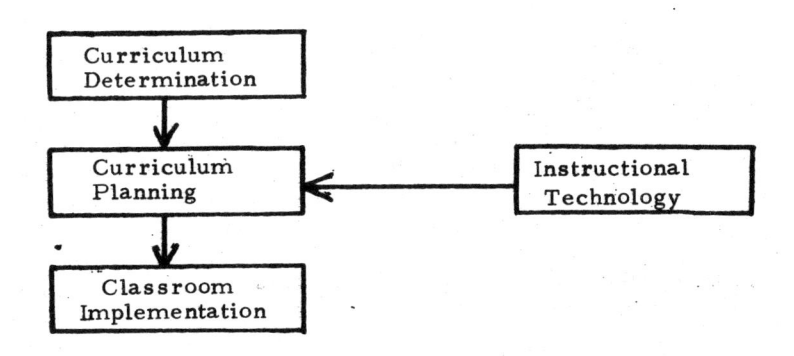

Fig. 2.--The Entry of Instructional Technology into the Instructional Process.

```
        ┌─────────────────┐
        │   Curriculum    │
        │  Determination  │
        └─────────────────┘
                 │
                 ▼
        ┌─────────────────┐
        │   Curriculum    │
        │    Planning     │
        │   (Strategy)    │
        └─────────────────┘
             │        │
             ▼        ▼
    ┌──────────┐  ┌──────────┐
    │ Mediated │  │Classroom │
    │Instruction│ │Instruction│
    └──────────┘  └──────────┘
```

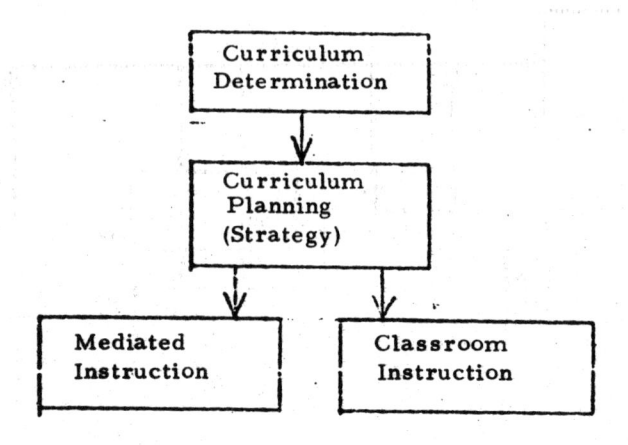

Fig. 3.--Two Broad Choices of Instructional Tactics

instructional activity which is being presented to the student via media.

As education moves toward becoming a part of technological culture, the instructional management becomes more complex in that increased changes in its basic structure will occur. The future trend will be toward an interaction between content, media, and methodology. More specifically, a team of media and classroom teachers, curriculum specialists, psychologists, and media specialists must work cooperatively at the curriculum planning level in order to come up with a decision in regard to packages for the use of mediated and classroom instruction, as illustrated in figure 4.

Any curriculum package at the local level of curriculum planning may be accepted or rejected. The classroom and mediated instruction will be set in motion in a joint enterprise if the package is accepted. Also, at any level, the recipients of instruction, the students, will be able to express themselves in regard to the quality of instruction they are receiving.

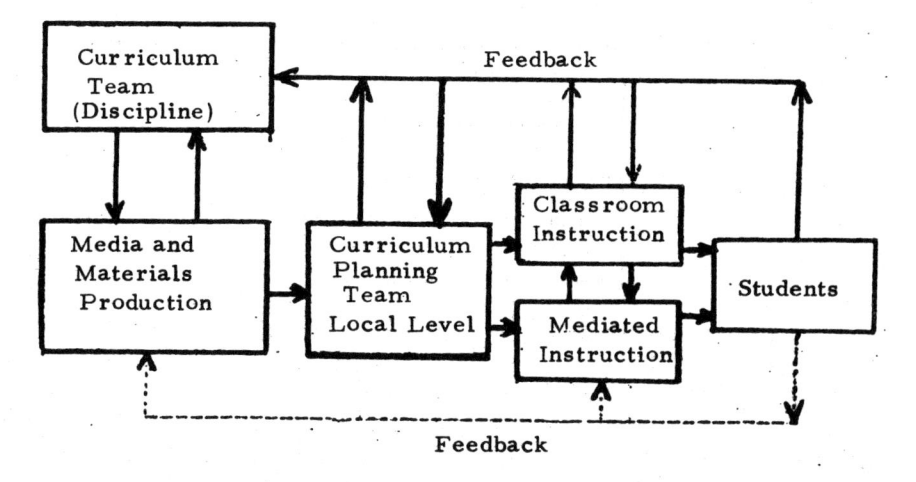

Fig. 4.--The Concept of Future Curriculum Construction

Learning Resources Unit and Staff Development

The overall educational quality may not be achieved without necessary human resource development. The main ingredient of staff development is an innovative leadership style exerted by the college chief executive. He must make efforts in order to acquaint the curriculum leaders and other administrators with the techniques and strategies of gathering, assessing, and sharing information in respect to instructional technology and student development resources. The data may be collected through reading; contacting commercial publishers; participating in workshops, professional organizations, meetings, and conventions; checking information through clearing houses; travel; academic exposure; and, surveying individuals or groups (16; 24).

One of the guidelines for two-year college Learning Resources programs indicates that:

> . . . professional development is the responsibility of both the institution and the professional staff member. Personal membership and participation in professional activities is

expected of all staff members. Further graduate study should be encouraged and rewarded. The institution is expected to encourage and support professional development by providing among other benefits: consultants for staff members and occasional attendance for every staff member at appropriate state or national meetings, workshops and seminars; and special arrangements for those staff members who serve as officers or committee members or participate on a state or national program. (1, pp. 57-58)

The contemporary Learning Resources Unit in comprehensive community junior colleges is a conglomerate of the library and the traditional audiovisual center. Its staff has as much responsibility for educating the heterogeneous character of community college students as the teaching faculty. In fact, Learning Resources programs, with their supportive function in institution-wide efforts, should "provide innovative leadership coupled with a multiplicity of varied resources which are managed by qualified staff who serve to facilitate the attainment of institutional objectives" (1, p. 51).

The success of Learning Resources programs depends upon meaningful involvement of Learning Resources staff with instructional administrative, and other staff members in the design, implementation, and evaluation of the overall educational programs of the institution. Likewise, the Learning Resources staff development contributes tremendously to attaining the institutional goals as well as to the staff members' personal and professional goals.

The main purpose of staff development in a Learning Resources unit is to obtain information which has immediate usefulness for transfer to the classroom. The staff development programs should therefore be designed in such manners that serve their purpose. Also, each staff member should evaluate his abilities to see what he could do differently for the students or in his instructional support as a result of participating in those programs (16; 17).

There are several approaches to staff development. First, skills development, in which the staff members acquire cognitive skills or techniques in order to be able to promote change. Second, consultation and discussion: in this approach self-examination and introspection are emphasized as processes for identifying both the desired direction and element of change. Third, adoption and implementation which pertain to a certain focus established by the desired materials, method, and technology. Fourth, personal and organizational development: both of these strategies operate on the same managing principle that the former may be achieved by facilatating the latter. Fifth, an evaluation and reward system: once a Learning Resources staff member or his counterpart in the instructional or administrative projects, as evaluated by the institution, he is ensured of resources as well as of tangible rewards. Sixth, comprehensive institutional development: which should encompass any or all of the above elements and is the strategy for the future. Its purpose is to serve the institutional goals as well as the professional goals of the faculty, administrators, Learning Resources and other staff members, and ultimately the students.

CHAPTER BIBLIOGRAPHY

[1] ACRL, AACJC, AECT, "Guidelines for Two-Year College Learning Resources Programs," Audiovisual Instruction 18 (January 1973):50-61.

[2] Buhl, Lance C., and Adele Greenfield, "Contracting for Professional Development in Academic," Educational Record 2 (Spring 1975):111-21.

[3] Butler, Broadus N., "Leadership Development in Higher Education," Educational Record 1 (Winter 1975):21-28.

[4] Buzzard, David and John R. Kinghorn, "To advise, You Must Communicate," The Clearing House 3 (November 1975): 100-103.

[5] Campbell, Clyde M., "Coordinating Leadership in Resource Use," Educational Leadership 30 (November 1972):110-12.

[6] Conte, Joseph M., and Fenwick English, "The Impact of Technology on Staff Differentiation," Audiovisual Instruction 14 (May 1969):108.

[7] Cyphert, Frederick R., and Ralph W. Ingersoll, "Leadership Strategy in Academic Administration," Journal of Teacher Education 4 (Winter 1974):357-59.

[8] Feltner, Bill D., "Training Programs for College Administration: Impact on Governance," Educational Record 3 (Summer 1975):156-59.

[9] Firth, Gerald R., "Theories of Leadership: Where Do We Stand?" Educational Leadership 5 (February 1976):327-31.

[10] Gibson, John T., "Power vs. Authority: Fundamentals of Leadership," The Clearing House 3 (November 1975):116-18.

[11] Hamreus, Dale G., "Media Guidelines," Audiovisual Instruction 15 (May 1970):31-34.

[12] Hanger, William S., and David G. Brown, "Pragmatics of Faculty Self-Development," Educational Record 3 (Summer 1975):201-206.

[13] Heinick, Robert, Technology and the Management of Instruction, Association for Educational Communications and Technology, 1970.

[14] Hoem, Eric, "The Professional Development Program You Can Afford," Community and Junior College Journal 47 (May 1975):32-34.

[15] Hoye, Robert E., "Systems Management," Audiovisual Instruction 20 (October 1975):6-7.

[16] Irwin, Judith T., ed., A Guide to Professional Development Opportunities for College and University Administrators, Washington Academy for Educational Development, Inc., and American Council on Education, 1975.

[17] Kirby, Paul W., "In-Service Education: The University's Role," Educational Leadership 30 (February 1973):431-33.

[18] McBeath, Ronald J., ed., Selected Writings by James D. Finn on Instructional Technology: Extending Education Through Technology, Association for Educational Communications and Technology, 1972.

[19] Miller, William A., Jr., A Monograph: Educational Planning and Program Management, North Texas State University Press, 1975.

[20] _____, A Monograph: Humanistic-Governance Management in Educational Administration, North Texas State University Press, 1975.

[21] _____, A Monograph: Leadership Style in Educational Administration, North Texas State University Press, 1975.

[22] Prigge, William C., "Media Management: A Quest for Quality," Audiovisual Instruction 20 (July 1975):3.

[23] Richman, Barry M., and Richard M. Farmer, Leadership, Goals, and Power in Higher Education, San Francisco, Jossey-Bass Publishers, Inc., 1974.

[24] Smith, M. F., "Collecting, Evaluating, Disseminating Information About Instructional Resources," Educational Leadership 30 (November 1972):113-15.

[25] Thomas, George, "Futuristics and Community College Planning," Community and Junior College Journal 45 (November 1974): 8-11.

CHAPTER III

THE LEARNING RESOURCE CENTER MANAGER AS AN EDUCATOR

Delois Smith

Preceding chapters have discussed leadership and management as essential tools for the achievement of effective and efficient administration of the learning resources center. The present chapter discusses in more detail some important concepts such as development, implementation, evaluation, selection of staff, planning, keeping staff informed and decision making. Multi-purpose, comprehensive, and inexpensive higher education is currently available in many localities for students with a diversity of ages and backgrounds. American higher education has faced an ever-increasing demand for its services and has begun to provide a solution.

The personality of higher education is shaped by the nature of its curriculum and instruction. If the institution is to be a dynamic forum for learning, then so must the curriculum and its instructional implementation. Higher education must commit itself to continuous self-examination, experimentation, and communication both within the institutional system and with the students for whom the system exists (7, p. 20).

The philosophy of institutions of higher education allow them to deal with the individual by offering a wide variety of programs. By implementing its comprehensive curriculum, higher education attempts to assist today's citizen toward a fuller realization of his potential. It is the goal of higher education to provide a responsive environment in which students and faculty can interact and freely grow, both emotionally and intellectually.

The learning resources center places primary emphasis upon meeting the needs of the students within a changing environment, the community.

The rationale for merging the library and audiovisual facilities into a single unit, the learning resources center, is based upon several assumptions. First, as society develops and grows more complex, no one particular format for communication can be considered as the most appropriate. Second, as materials and services become more accessible, the potential for learning becomes greater. The recent recommendations of the survey on institutions of higher education in the state of Illinois indicate that "the learning resources center should be administered as one unit under a single director (10, p. 1). The survey also states that 75.5 percent of the participating colleges were currently administering the library and audiovisual services as a single unit (10, p. 10). Therefore, combined services with a single head, the director of learning resources, an interfiled main card catalog, and close proximity of print and nonprint materials indicate that the learning resources center concept is being adopted by institutions of higher education because better services are provided for students and faculty if all media are coordinated and administered by one department. Third, a very practical factor is that of control. Many colleges which have not adopted a single administrative unit have found their materials and equipment scattered throughout the complex, leading to much duplication and lack of accessibility by students and faculty (10, p. 12).

The learning resources center has two primary functions, service and instruction. Service involves the provision of whatever materials, equipment, assistance, and guidance are required by the user. The function of instruction is implemented through assisting the student to inquire, to search, and to find a commitment to make his true education a reality. The faculty has to be aware of the opportunities available to their students and themselves through a unified facility. The more knowledge and understanding the students and faculty have of the learning resources center facilities, the more likely they will utilize and rely upon its resources.

The director of the learning resources center and his staff have an additional duty of teaching students and faculty how to search for and use all the media that has been coordinated into one effective unit, the learning resources center. It is a continuous process that requires time, patience, understanding of faculty and students, a good knowledge of curriculum and good professional personnel (2, pp. 12-14).

The nature of the services and the scope of the services to be implemented by the learning resources center will be affected by the organization of the administrative unit. The center should have as its chief administrator a person who is knowledgeable in at least four areas: library, audio-visual, curriculum, and management. The problems which will confront this unit will be of such a nature that a background of training and experience in these areas will be a necessity. T. N. Duprey has listed three principal problem areas as the following:

1. The first concerns structure, coordination of activities, and functional relationships within the learning resources center and other activities on the campus.
2. The proper use and coordination of non-book media with book media in the learning process.
3. There are few trained specialists who are also good managers with knowledge, experience and understanding of both areas. (5, p. 59)

The dean or director of learning resources usually is responsible to the dean or vice president of instruction. If the institution is administratively organized with a vice president in charge of instruction, then the chief administrator of the learning resources center would be a dean; however, if the instruction is organized with a dean of instruction, the chief administrative officer of the learning resources center would probably be called a director.

A common practice in higher education is to set up an advisory committee for the learning resources center. It is the duty of this committee to represent the different divisions of the institution and the student body, thus allowing one channel of communication between these forces and the center. It is recommended that at least one student serve on the advisory committee. The director may serve as committee chairman. Alternative methods for establishing the committee may include: appointment by the president; appointment by the dean; election or appointment by the faculty, either directly or through a faculty committee or selection by the head of the learning resources center. The function of the committee is advisory and it is important that the committee does not concern itself with the details of daily administration.

The self-instructional laboratory, as one unit of the center, is directly responsible to the dean or director. The independent study concept is receiving increased attention in institutions of higher education. One phase of this concept is a laboratory where students can utilize materials and equipment for individualized learning. The direction of this laboratory should be under a person with knowledge in the areas of both print and nonprint media, since a variety of materials will be utilized for effective integration of curricular needs. The self-instructional laboratory should be housed as a part of the center for easy access by both students and faculty, and should be staffed by teaching personnel from the different disciplines as well as paraprofessional staff. In many cases this area is coordinated and integrated with a diagnostic center for learning difficulties.

Both the coordinator of library services and the coordinator of audiovisual services should be under direct supervision of the director. Both have total responsibility for their respective areas and have parallel positions in the organizational scheme. For the total development of the learning resources center concept, the coordinators of both areas must work cooperatively in achieving the objectives of the center. Some institutions have totally merged the responsibilities and have not separated the traditional audiovisual and library services in the learning resources center: for instance, technical services include both print and nonprint materials, and circulation includes all materials and equipment. The intershelving of all items in the center may require alternative organization structures.

The coordinator of audio-visual services is responsible for the organization and administration of duplicating services, instructional television, the production of nonprint materials, and the distribution of nonprint materials and equipment. In some instances the instructional television facility may be separate from the audiovisual facility and equal to it in line relationship, depending upon the size of the institution and the emphasis placed upon it. Two auxiliary services, because of their relationship to the audiovisual complex, are the language laboratory and the reading laboratory. It is recommended that these units be coordinated and located within the learning resources center since the production of materials and maintenance of equipment are vital functions in their effective operation.

The coordinator of library services has as his responsibility the administration and operation of the library, including the acquisition, cataloging and circulation of print and nonprint materials. Reference and technical services, circulation and acquisitions, and serials activities are under his direct supervision. Another duty of the library coordinator is the maintenance of a faculty library. It is his responsibility to see that appropriate materials are purchased and processed for the faculty.

Many colleges are implementing curricula designed to train audiovisual and library technicians. The responsibilities of initiating and administering such a program can fall within the realm of the dean of instruction and be delegated to the director of the learning resources center. While nationally there is concern for the administration of these programs, it is recommended that the learning resources center be given responsibility for directing these programs and that a cooperative spirit exist to allow the students to receive the most appropriate learning experiences. The center itself serves as an excellent laboratory for the students to gain practical on-the-job experience (2, pp. 20-32).

The efficiency and success of the learning resources center in meeting its desired goals will be dependent upon the quality of staff it employs, and upon the internal and external communication system that is established throughout the organization. "The unique task of administration, at least with respect to staff relations, is just this: to integrate the demands of the staff members in a way that is organizationally productive and individually fulfilling" (6, p. 430).

The principles of management are essential in the attainment of a common goal within the institution. It is the responsibility of the president, the dean, the director, and also the technician.

Henri Fayol has listed fourteen principles of management which can serve as a guideline for effective operation. They are as follows:

1. Division of work
2. Authority and Responsibility
3. Disciple
4. Unity of Command
5. Unity of Direction
6. Subordination
7. Remunerarion
8. Centralization
9. Scalar Chain

10. Order
11. Equity
12. Stability of Tenure
13. Initiative
14. Esprit de Corps   (6, pp. 18-19)

The work of the organization is carried out through effective communication. The communicative channels not only flow downward but upward and horizontally. Communication is based upon trust. The lack of the concept of trust can keep subordinates from communicating with their supervisor and inhibit the process. If a mutual understanding and cooperation exists, then barriers will be reduced or minimized. However, in every organization some barriers will still be present. To minimize these restrictions the following factors should be considered: (1) preventing downward channels of communication from being overloaded; (2) encouraging the free flow of ideas and information in all directions; (3) developing a sensitivity among members of the administrative staff to the need for understanding the psychological barriers to effective communication; and, (4) planning programs to help members of the administrative staff with some of the fundamental problems of communication with which they are confronted (4, p. 63). Instead of always referring decisions to the top of the organization, the collective group can and should be involved in the communication process. For example, general functions which groups might perform include the following: planning, appraising, advising, and educating. "Group productivity depends upon many things, including the competency of its members, the nature of the task with which it is confronted, the processes employed in the conduct of the work, the extent to which groups are permitted to use initiative in solving problems, and administrative integrity in dealing with group suggestions, decisions, or recommendations" (4, p. 69).

The learning resources center requires a broadly educated and well-qualified staff in the area of communication. Familiarity with both print and non-print media and their implications and effectiveness in the process of communication is a necessity.

To date, the position of director of a community college learning resources center or of an institution of higher education is usually filled by a person from the library field since most administrators still perceive the library as a necessary but traditional fixture on the college campus. The director should be a knowledgeable person in both areas, that of library and audiovisual.

The specialist should have the following backgrounds:

1. Have a knowledge of curriculum theory and of the dynamics of curriculum change and development.
2. Have a background of successful teaching.
3. Be able to communicate ideas clearly.
4. Be able to delegate responsibilities.
5. Have the ability to initiate interaction.
6. Be a communicator, interpreter, and promoter of research.
7. Have a knowledge of classification and cataloging procedures and the ability to implement them.
8. Be professionally prepared and aggressive enough to acquire that status . . . .
9. Maintain intellectual curiosity and display a willingness to keep abreast of new developments . . . .
10. Have a knowledge of building design and facilities . . . .
11. Be able to work effectively with individuals and with groups. (12, pp. 17-18)

Thus, the director needs to be a leader and a communicator with knowledge areas in the field of curriculum theory, communication, library, audiovisual, and learning theory. He also needs to know how to work with others and to gain their respect.

James Brown (3, p. 23) has indicated that a media generalist could provide leadership in the area. This generalist would have the following qualifications:

1. A professional resource person for teachers first and foremost; for media center professional and paraprofessional staff, for administrators, and for students
2. A knowledgeable curriculum worker
3. An administrator
4. A professional practitioner
5. A catalyst for innovation and for the extension of practices of proven worth, a student of the process of educational change and especially of human relations and motivations

A Walter Stone (16, pp. 182-83) in a recent issue of Library Trends, stated:

> In the future, competence of those performing the library function will no longer be measured in terms of specific media backgrounds as such but in terms of subject mastery and communications expertise. Needed in the future to manage library services will be several new classes of personnel including specialists in communications analysis, production, packaging, and evaluation; systems designers and analysts; and dynamic distributive program administrators. All must be thoroughly familiar with ways in which the various forms of recorded knowledge can be acquired, stored, retrieved, distributed, and used with maximum effectiveness.

In these areas, Wyman (21, p. 116) has addressed himself to the question by asking "Whose Empire?" We do need two new professional people who have not yet appeared on the scene in any appreciable numbers. We need a specialist in presentation design and techniques. Audiovisual people would most likely move into the presentation area as they learned about producing presentations, group dynamics, research deisgn, room construction, etc. Librarians would most likely move into the individual study area as they learned more about newer media used in individual study carrels, evaluation, guidance, particularly programmed instruction.

The director's primary responsibility is the administration and integration of the learning resources center with the institution's objectives. One of the director's roles is the supervision of professional, paraprofessional and clerical staff.

The staff of the learning resources center can be divided into two categories. Although persons in both categories share some duties, the responsibility factor will vary considerably. The professional staff includes those persons who have advanced degrees, have considerable responsibility, understand the objectives, functions and operations of the unit, and are involved in an instructional position.

Professional media specialists are generally acknowledged to be professionals by their relationship to the main task, instruction not by their relationship to media.

The librarian has to be a teacher for while he is managing he is also involved vitally in instruction. Through his efforts he coordinates the efforts of the faculty and the available resources into a single unit. Unfortunately, the librarian may forget his role in instruction and allocate more time to administration duties.

Most librarians are overburdened with administrative detail. They have to cover the real administrative functions: formulating overall objectives and policies; planning; determining the organizational framework; making major decisions, including those on personnel; supervising the "middle management" heads, and seeing that they carry well the responsibilities delegated to them; balancing and coordinating all the workers and activities into a smoothly operating whole, and evaluating what is going on (20, p. 72).

Some necessary attributes for the librarian are: a fundamental knowledge of librarianship; knowledge of the higher education movement; successful teaching experience; and, a willingness and cooperative attitude toward faculty, students, and other staff members of the center. The position requires delegation and supervision. The librarian needs the qualities of leadership, good judgment, initiative, intellectual curiosity, and resourcefulness. The success or failure of the person will be largely determined by his successful or unsuccessful efforts in working with others inside and outside the center.

The trained paraprofessional is another element of the library staff and includes those persons referred to as the "library assistant" and the "technical assistant." The library assistant usually has a four-year degree and duties which may vary considerably. The library technical assistant performs diverse tasks. An understanding of the functions of the operation of the center and the knowledge to respond to users' requests are a necessity for the technician.

The audiovisual personnel consist of professional and technical.

"The fundamental responsibilities of the media specialist or district director are divided into three areas: administrative, supervisory, and technical" (17, p. 25). "The media man's activities in other areas will result in a necessary relignment of relationships with other personnel, especially other administrators: administrative arrangements must be made to permit operation within the previously mentioned areas, and in addition to such policies or operating procedures, the media man must prove he is competent not only in the area of media, but also in curriculum, learning, and supervision" (8, p. 29). The relationships tend to be shifted from the internal organization, the center, to external, the campus community. A major consideration becomes learning and not an organizational hierarchy of personnel. This is not to say that proper organization arrangements are unnecessary, but learning and instruction are paramount in the institutions of higher education.

Dale Hamreus (9, p. 32) has proposed a three-dimensional structure for organizing media-related training requirements. One of the dimensions is aligned to responsibilities that media personnel assume in performing their duties and is thus designated as responsibility grouping.

The directive-administrative grouping includes job activities that represent top administrative and management responsibilities necessary to control media operations; the professional grouping includes job activities that are responsible to work directly in the use of media with learners and learning problems, e.g., teachers and instructional designers, etc., the artistic-production grouping represents job activities that are responsible to work directly in the creation and production of media in support of professional type activities, e.g., graphic artist, photographer, etc. The technical grouping represents job activities that are responsible to work directly with the design, fabrication, technical adjustment, and operation of mediating devices required in instruction in support of the professional type activities, e.g. TV camermen, technical professor, etc.

To fulfill his responsibility, the media person must spend his time working with classroom teachers in selecting materials and effective utilization of these materials.

A professional audiovisualist needs to understand the process of communication, teaching, supervision, learning theory, curriculum, and the audiovisual field.

The technician in the audiovisual field has received considerable attention focused upon his duties and his training. He is a necessity within the organizational structure of the learning resources center. The technician's duties consist of the following: (1) interviews, hires, and trains student assistants in the use of audiovisual equipment and location of materials; (2) operates videotape equipment and distribution of audio and video signals throughout the campus-wide closed-circuit television network and learning center; (3) schedules and supervises delivery and pick-up of equipment; and, (4) prepares and reproduces instructional materials (13, p. 73).

Elwood Miller (15, p. 60) has noted that the technician must be able to communicate and work with trained professionals and therefore should have a good command of language and communications tools. His training might include a) operation and use of equipment, b) simple maintenance, c) knowledge of materials services, d) production of basic graphics for television, e) knowledge of photography f) knowledge of lighting, floor direction, camera work, and prop construction, and g) audio work necessary for production of sound tapes.

In order to provide the technician with some knowledge of the educational situation in institutions of higher education, his audiovisual training should commence and terminate at the college in an audiovisual technician curriculum. Primary objectives of a program would include: an understanding of basic mass communication patterns along with electronic and engineering knowledge to support a system, an understanding of basic production techniques and an understanding of data processing, programmed instruction, technology, and television in order to work with others in an intelligent and productive manner (14, p. 62).

Students are a most important category of assistants. They are used for many tasks since they bring to work a wide variety of their skills and experiences. They may be found in any unit of the Learning Resources Center in technical and public services. In practically all libraries they are either responsible for or assist with shelving. They may be found at circulation counters issuing books; they may be stationed in catalog and order departments assisting with typing or marking books; they may assist in bibliographic checking; they are often responsible for transporting audiovisual equipment and for operating various kinds of projectors and other devices. In recent years the federal government has made available funds to employ students on the work-study program. Students can contribute in many areas to the successful operation of the Learning Resources Center. They are likely to attract other fellow students to learning centers. They may view their involvement with the library in such a positive fashion that they may wish to make learning resources a career and become either professional or supportive staff members (18, pp. 376-79).

The success of the learning resources center in meeting the instructional objectives will depend upon the personnel and the proper administration of resources. The administrator of the center who does not consider, or is not aware of, the principles of management will have more difficulty in obtaining a cooperative and unified effort. The individual within the organization must realize his own worth to the organization and be allowed to fulfill his role.

Evaluation cannot precede program, but program must be preceded by plan; and the plan must recognize two essentials: First, that any learning resource program must be organized in terms of the needs of a particular institution; second, that the program must be flexible and adaptable to new needs as they develop (1, p. 11).

There is provision for continuous evaluation of the higher education library program by means of appropriate techniques and measures.

The dynamic nature of institutions of higher education makes continuous evaluation of the individual curricula, objectives and functions necessary. As they are revised, the library program should reflect the changes.

Quantitative measures and statistics have significance when applied flexibly, realistically, and in balance with qualitative considerations. These continue to be effective in helping library and college administrators see their libraries realistically, by indicating areas where improvement is needed. Also they have been especially important and useful in areas of library personnel, collection, finances, quarters and equipment.

A continuous evaluation of the library's contribution to the higher education program can be a cooperative endeavor of the professional library staff and other faculty. An advisory library committee can, under certain circumstances, be a force for continuous evaluation of library resources and services.

Some illustrative measures of the second criterion are:

1. A library consultant is employed in preplanning.
2. The current library program has been evaluated by a library consultant whose report consists of a professional library survey, the results of which are being published and implemented.
3. Guidelines for evaluation provided by the "ALA Standards for Junior College Libraries" are utilized.
4. Specific recommendations of accrediting or supervisory agencies have been published and are being carried out.

Recognition of the utility of the ALA Standards by the library directors is significant, for it means that there is some provision for continuous evaluation of most institutions of higher education library programs by means of appropriate techniques and measures.

Statements by the library directors reveal mixed reactions as to the application of the Standards, however. For example: (1) the criticisms made by the AAJC Commission on Administration reveal an alarming lack of knowledge of college library functions and confusion with high school on the part of the presidents and administrators; (2) pressure on governing boards and administrators from outside the college is needed to raise library standards; (3) librarians try to get the Standards over to administration and get nowhere until much later, (accreditation) recommendations are along more or less the same lines; (4) the problem is to get administrative support--they consider state and regional standards; (5) minimum standards are useful only when they are interpreted as general guidelines for the resources needed to meet the minimum needs of an average institution-specialized curricula demand for more library materials; and, (6) a capable librarian and an ALA Standard-budget are all that are needed (1, pp. 14-18).

Until the library directors are able to communicate to their chief administrators their belief in the value of the ALA Standards, the funds necessary for implementation will not be forthcoming. The fact that accrediting bodies ultimately make recommendations along similar lines does not diminish the alarming implications of the situation, for the ALA Standards are basically planning guidelines, whereas accrediting recommendations are commentaries on existing inadequacies.

Currently library programs are not often evaluated by means of the professional library survey, possibly because this usually involves an expenditure for the service itself and the implementation of recommendations. In the long run, recommendations which are implemented are those made by college accrediting or supervisory agencies, 60.1% of the library programs having received specific recommendations. Accrediting and supervisory agencies' most frequent recommendations are: increased library facilities, especially seating; increased library staff, especially librarians; increased collection, referring to quantity rather than quality; increased library budget and increased library use by faculty (19, pp. 11, 29-32).

To evaluate and improve the effectiveness of the Learning Resources Program:

1. Utilize state and national standards for periodic evaluation.
2. Develop and make use of an instrument for the evaluation of the library services.
3. Make operational and policy changes should the need be indicated as a result of evaluation responses.
4. Solicit suggestions from the Learning Resources Committee.

Instructional Media

1. An evaluation form will accompany all locally produced materials delivered to faculty.
2. An evaluation form will be provided for all equipment and materials set up for classroom use.
3. Maintain record of evaluation responses.
4. Make operational and policy changes should the need be indicated as a result of evaluation responses (11, pp. 10-12)

The learning resource center does not exist in a vacuum, but it is shaped by the goals and objectives of the institution of which it is a part and also by outside forces and development affecting education and librarianship.

Administrators in higher education who are sensitive to changing educational and occupational needs of our society, will adapt curricula and resources to meet the new challenges.

CHAPTER BILBIOGRAPHY

[1] Adams, Harlen, The Junior College Library Program, A Study of Library Services in Relation to Instructional Procedures, American Library Association, Chicago, 1940.

[2] Allen, Kenneth W., and Loren Allen, Organization and Administration of the Learning Resources Center in the Community College and in Institutions of Higher Education, Shoe String Press, Connecticut, 1973.

[3] Brown, James W., "AV and Library: Complement or Merge?" Educational Screen and Audio-Visual Guide 46 (January 1967).

[4] Castetter, William B., Administering the School Personnel Program, Macmillan Co., New York, 1962.

[5] Duprey, T. N., The Impact of Information Technology, Communication Service Corporation, Washington, 1968.

[6] Getzels, J. W., and E. G. Guba, "Social Behavior and the Administrative Process," The School Review, 45 (Winter 1967)

[7] Glenzer, Edmund, This Is the Community College, Houghton Mifflin, Boston, 1968.

[8] Grady, Bill F., "The Preparation and Certification of Educational Media Personnel," Audiovisual Instruction 14 (January 1969).

[9] Hamreus, Dale, "Media Guidelines," Audiovisual Instruction 15 (May 1970).

[10] Illinois Library Association, A Multimedia Survey of Community College and Institutions of Higher Education Libraries of the State of Illinois, Illinois Library Association, Chicago, 1970.

[11] Learning Resources Operational Model Tarrant County Junior College, South Campus, 1972.

[12] Lewis Philip, "The Role of the Educational Communications Specialists," American School Board Journal 143 (December 1961).

[13] Meyers, Richard S., "Money and Morale," Audiovisual Instruction 15 (May 1970).

[14] _____., "Community College Media Technology Program," Audiovisual Instruction 14 (September 1969).

[15] Miller, Elwood, "Proposed: A Media Clerk-Technician," Audiovisual Instruction 9 (November 1964).

[16] Stone, Walter C., "The Library Function Redefined," Library Trends 16 (October 1967).

[17] Veit, Fritz, "Job Descriptions for Library Technical Assistants," Council on Library Technology, Chicago, 1970.

[18] _____, The Community College Library, Greenwood Press, Connecticut, 1975.

[19] Wheeler, Helen, The Community College Library: A Plan for Action, Shoe String Press, Connecticut, 1965.

[20] Wheeler, Joseph, and Herbert Goldhor, Practical Administration of Public Libraries, Harper and Row, New York, 1962.

[21] Wyman, Raymond, "The Instructional Materials Center: Whose Empire?" Audiovisual Instruction 12 (February 1967).

CHAPTER IV

ROLE AND RESPONSIBILITY OF LEARNING RESOURCE CENTER MANAGERS

Larry Hunt

Since the media center is an integral part of the college's education and administrative structure, it reflects different levels of emphasis upon particular program elements related to the college's mission. The center provides direct service to students and faculty. It provides media collections, and development of these collections, assists in creating instructional design that fulfills the educational goals of the school, and conducts staff development activities.

The media center functions under the leadership of a director --usually a media professional with a knowledge of education and with management competencies. He is charged with the responsibility of implementing the overall policies related to the college, and must operate the center in accordance with the educational philosophies of the college district. How should the director see his role? He should see himself first as an educator, providing those services which will assist his clients educationally. He should be an administrator and deal with his staff in a proficient and competent manner. His professional skills should be such that he can be a consultant to his staff, and provide technical expertise related to media.

Erickson (5, p. 31) lists the specific duties and responsibilities of the learning resources director as follows:

1. Provision for clerical and technical help in keeping all equipment and materials readily accessible to all faculty.
2. Making periodic inventories of equipment and materials.
3. Preparation of reports for the administration on the status and needs of audio-visual services.
4. Involvement of teachers in the actual selection of materials and equipment.
5. Keeping faculty informed of new acquisitions, materials, film confirmations, and pending equipment purchases.
6. Regular checking of equipment and materials to determine that all items are serviceable and in working order.

7. Maintaining records on equipment usage, and costs.
8. Serving the president and deans of the college as a consultant in the area of materials and equipment.
9. Providing facilities and/or opportunities for professional development or in-service training for faculty.
10. Providing for the classifying and cataloging of a wide variety of materials.
11. Providing for making minor repairs, servicing, and replacement of parts.
12. Utilizing training opportunities for faculty, students, and technical personnel in the operation and care of equipment.
13. Providing facilities and consultative services to faculty and/or pupils in arranging preview sessions for films, filmstrips, etc.
14. Provision for the acquisition of free and rental materials for faculty.
15. Serving as a consultant on matters of improving physical facilities of classrooms in matters of acoustics, light control, room darkening or ventilation.
16. Provision for the repair and/or servicing of equipment.
17. Involving teachers in establishing criteria for the selection of audio-visual materials and equipment.
18. Assisting in the preparation of handbooks for teachers which describe the services of the center.
19. Providing equipment and materials for special classes such as foreign language departments, etc.
20. Serving as a consultant on matters of providing information about equipment ratios and/or standards.
21. Providing equipment and materials for special classes such as special education classes, etc.
22. Making available an extensive selection of audiovisual books and magazines as a professional library for faculty and other personnel.
23. Providing facilities and consultative assistance to instructors and pupils in planning the utilization of materials and equipment.
24. Provision for the regular checking of sources of indexes of enrichment materials.
25. Providing student operators for equipment operation in classrooms.
26. Serving as a consultant or advisor on matters of curriculum revision and development.

27. Providing facilities and opportunities for the audio-visual in-service training for faculty members, and demonstrating the preparation and use of materials.
28. Prividing facilities and consultative assistance to faculty and students in arranging demonstrations and doing demonstrations when invited.
29. Encouraging and stimulating faculty to develop a high degree of audio-visual competencies.
30. Providing facilities and opportunities for individual conferences with teachers on audio-visual problems.
31. Providing publicity through appropriate media about the activities and services of the audio-visual center.
32. Assisting faculty and/or students in the preparation and production of audio-visual materials. (5, p. 31)

In most schools, universities or colleges there are organizational charts and job descriptions that place the director in the administrative organizational structure. The main considerations are concerned with the director being close to policy-forming levels of action, whether or not he is close to curriculum leaders and other key administrative personnel in promoting needed changes, and whether or not the media program director may concentrate his time and energies on media-development problems.

In most cases the media director should be placed at the highest possible point in the administrative and instructional hierarchy that permits him to work coordinately with other leaders, but under director authority of the chief educational decision maker. He should be in a position to direct all his efforts to the media development programs.

Administrative and Staff Development

What makes the difference between a very competent media staff, and one which is of average competence? What makes some people perform in an effective manner--able to make complex decisions? Why do some people always seem to be in the right place at the right time? Why do some professionals seem to be confident in their role, and others seem to be much less sure?

In addition to basic differences in abilities and capabilities, part of the answer to the above may be answered in terms of professional development. It is important for the media director to be not only an expert in media technology, but also in education and human development. Without administrative leadership abilities, technological knowledge and skill in teaching, his action will be minimized, he will be unable to develop plans and proposals in terms of educational impact, and his ability to anticipate difficulties and make a number of other judgments about such matters as cost and needed facilities for group and individual responses, is likely to be so underdeveloped that serious errors are almost sure to be made.

To be successful, the media center staff must be flexible and adaptable to change. Getting people to learn new ideas, getting people to put old ideas to work with new tools, getting people to use commonly available devices and instruments in entirely new ways and in new configurations is the process of change in action. Fortunately there is such a thing as a "change agent"--the innovative personality.

Where does the media program director and his staff fit into the change process? What changes can he make? He can order no changes for instructors or deans to implement, no major policy or procedural changes dealing with philosophy. He can, however, create changes in his own procedure and he can influence other administrators to support his porposals. Thus, he becomes an originator of ideas that he initiates for others, and places at their disposition for use.

In face of constant change, what responses are required of those directors who are sensitive to change?

1. The director must discover educational needs and problems that instructors face in daily classroom activity--doing this by means of surveys, observations, and reports. Such findings, knowledge, and skill can be brought to focus on evaluation, need, and scope of change.
2. Identify special needs of a global nature, mapping out plans of action in broad outline form, and preparing proposals in detail for possible implementation by the administration.

Because of the constant pressure for change on the media center director, he must provide for continuing activities which will develop professional competencies within his staff. Not only should staff members be aware of technological developments, but they should become aware of their strengths and weaknesses in dealing with people and serving the public.

Acquisition of Media

The media director must bear the responsibility of deciding what to buy, but those who are to use the equipment deserve the right to participate in decision making. In inviting and encouraging involvement (perhaps through an equipment committee) the director uses his own specially developed powers of observation in acting as a leader of the group. Working with a director, an equipment committee might be composed of an adult or continuous education instructor or faculty member in various disciplines, and should be able to come to sound decisions on critical equipment problems. The director should encourage this sort of participation. Should the committee support a decision which the director opposes, he should be open-minded enough to accept the recommendation as an alternative and utilize the decision making process in choosing the best alternative, then execute it to the best of his ability. The director must realize that pressures to purchase a specific brand of media equipment may be intense. Many times local and regional distributors can muster strong forces within a community that can result in extremely embarrassing situations. Therefore there is a significant advantage in a pooled judgment, using all the facts that can be gained from representative participation by skilled observers in competitive demonstrations.*

In addition to the job of evaluation and selection of specific brands, the equipment committee should chart an operational plan for handling of media equipment problems.

As the committee makes its selection, there are several standards of general nature that may be used to good advantage.

1. Portability.--Is the piece of equipment easy to handle and move around? Is it reasonably light in weight in

---

*From ADMINISTERING EDUCATIONAL MEDIA, Copyright 1965, McGraw-Hill Book Company. Used with permission of McGraw-Hill Book Company

comparison to others? Is it compact? Are handles placed conveniently for easy carrying? Of course, for large pieces of equipment that are to be stored permanently or semi-permanently, this standard would not apply.
2. Ruggedness.--Will this piece of equipment give good operating service with a minimum trouble? Is it free of vibration during operation? Are the joints, supports, braces, and connections tight and strong? Are the carrying handles securely attached?
3. Cost.--In comparison with other brands or kinds of equipment, and in terms of other criteria, is the cost reasonable and competitive?
4. Ease of operation.--Can faculty and students operate the equipment effectively? In general, is the equipment easy to use? Are the control mechanisms few in number?
5. Quality of Performance.--How well does the equipment meet desirable performance standards? Can the equipment be depended upon to perform at desirable levels consistently?
6. Effective Design.--Is the design attractive? Is it free of imperfections and errors in construction? Is it free of unfinished or rough exterior parts? Is the finish functional and attractive? Is the finish easily marred? Was the equipment designed with school use in mind? Does the equipment include appropriate safety features?
7. Ease of Maintenance and Repair.--Can necessary minor adjustments be made easily and quickly? Are parts that need cleaning frequently conveniently accessible? Are the parts standard and easily available for purchase? Is it easy to remove the sections likely to need repair, that is, without complete disassembly?
8. Reputation of Manufacturer.--Is production of school equipment a major concern of the company? Is the research, planning, and development record of the company favorable? Is it likely that the company will continue in business for the school field?
9. Local Equipment Status.--Is it worthwhile to switch to new equipment when switching means replacement of all similar units presently used?
10. Available Service.--Are repair and emergency service facilities nearby? Are adequate stocks of spare parts maintained locally? (2, p. 75)

Distribution of Media Systems

Delivery systems are the means by which students and teachers obtain materials, equipment, and other resources at the time of need or desire. Each system must develop its own structure and definition, but creative organization and skill must be developed to fit every organization. Torkelson (9) lists certain basic principles that should be applied to distribution of media at each center.

1. Processing services provide efficient acquisition and organization of materials for accessibility to users.
2. Retrieval systems - cataloging, indexing, and remote access retrieval, facilitate use of all information in the school and district collections.
3. Access to information sources beyond the college is provided by such means as cooperative arrangements with community agencies.
4. Principles of cost-effectiveness are used in determining the best levels and locations--classroom, school media center, etc.--at which to provide media for various purposes.
5. Access to a variety of materials gives the user opportunity to grow in ability to make choices, compare ideas, and discover new interest.
6. The media program provides opportunities for the student to learn how to make self-directed searches for knowledge.
7. The test of any delivery system is how well it provides convenient, flexible, and speedy access to all media (9, p. 199)

Facility Design and Utilization

In view of the existing need for new construction and for remodeling old structures, the prospective media center director must prepare himself to take proper action in determining precisely what instructors need and utilize in their classroom and other learning areas to facilitate the use of the required media. Although the media director's knowledge of construction may make him an authority on the subject, he need not be an architect. He needs to be capable, however, of advising the administration and architect accurately on what the media-use requirements are, and he ought to be able to examine preliminary plans to see that the recommendations have been incorporated correctly into the construction design. A great deal of abuse has been directed toward some architects for their designs of buildings that showed little concern for the contemporary use of essential audiovisual media equipment and materials. Such criticism should have been more properly directed to college administrators and laymen who couldn't make up their minds what they wanted and needed. It doesn't seem likely that an architect will defy a board of regents' requests and specifications and attempt to force it to accept what it doesn't want. There is substantial agreement today as to the physical facilities that will make possible the efficient utilization of instructional technology, and it is up to the prospective director to become familiar with various alternatives and to make wise recommendations in terms of local conditions.

Increasing emphasis needs to be given to the principle that media-use facilities are needed in each of the learning spaces where the instructional tasks are being normally and naturally performed. This means that media are needed in libraries, conventional, large-group learning areas, special and general laboratory spaces, and in gymnasiums and auditoriums as well. It is inefficient and distracting to move a class of learners to a projections room, for example, in order to view a filmstrip or a motion picture, or to evict an instructor from his customary classroom to let another teacher use it. Students need to be able to respond to media used in combination and in depth with a minimum of distraction, and it is understandable that when instructors carry, push, and drag equipment units into position and return them on inconvenient schedules, their own professional work suffers. Consequently media may be inefficiently and ineffectively used, or not used at all.

A sustained effort should be maintained by the director of the media services program in arranging for adequate physical facilities and the required equipment in the construction and equipment plans for every new building. If this is not done, the job of equipping classrooms in older buildings may prove to be costly and inefficient.

Production

The school media program is concerned with production by

the media staff, teachers, aides, students, and even by people from the community. It offers opportunities for the creation, adaptation, and duplication of materials needed by instructors and students not readily or economically available elsewhere. The media staff provides and maintains convenient work areas, engages in production, and gives consultative and technical assistance to production projects.

When practical, a production activity in a given format may be centered at an individual school for its own or for multi-school use: for example, a large college will make extensive use of closed-circuit television programming, or vocational-technical divisions may offer advanced printing-trades curricula. Colleges with technicians skilled in producing working models may offer to share these capabilities, and institutions with learning programs that stress manual competencies may offer a variety of production services.

The college media program provides the following minimum production capabilities:

Graphics: the preparation of visuals, including dry mounting, laminating, and transparency production.

Photography: facilities and equipment for black-and-white photography, 2" x 2" color slides, and silent 8mm motion film photography.

Television and radio: the production of videotape recordings.

Audiotape production: the recording and duplication of audiotapes.

Insofar as possible, all facilities, equipment, supplies, and professional and technical assistance are available for student use. Student production occurs as a natural component of the educational experience and develops capabilities to translate elements of the environment into meaning modes of communication. Creating materials in all formats sharpens the student's critical response to media, expands dialogue and the transmission of ideas, and fosters growth in precise and effective written and oral expression. The quality of all production aspects is most important in the media center.

Maintenance

Maintenance extends from repairing cords of projectors and spines of books to nonfunctioning projectors and tape recorders. Its purposes are dual: good maintenance contributes largely to the comfort and efficiency of learners, teachers, and staff; it also plays an important part in economical and efficient management.

Some guidelines that apply to the area of maintenance are:

1. Preventative maintenance insures longer life of materials and equipment.

2. All types of materials and equipment should be inspected periodically to prevent, detect, and repair damage.

3. Budget provisions should be made for replacement of worn materials unsuitable for repair and of items of equipment for which maintenance costs exceed replacement costs.

The appearance of the media center should reflect long range maintenance and daily care.

The collection of materials and equipment should always be in good condition; items in the media center should be competently maintained and immediately ready for use.

Media staff should perform preventive maintenance by such tasks as reinforcing and repairing materials, changing lamps and fuses, and regularly inspecting and cleaning equipment. Users are encouraged to report any damages and malfunctions they observe. To avoid both the necessity for repairs and the possibility of user frustration, items requiring special precautions are identified by labels. Instruction in use of materials and equipment should emphasize proper handling and care of collections.

Continuous checking of the condition of materials and equipment within the collection is an established part of the media circulation system. In addition, systematic inspection must be scheduled at regular intervals.

Records of equipment usage and maintenance provide data for analyzing the cost-effectiveness of given items, and the media director creates such forms or delegates and directs the heads of various functions to set up record-keeping systems. These records are used as a basis for making decisions to replace items of equipment for which repair costs become excessive.

The director of the center plans maintenance procedures according to the policy of the college district and the services it provides for major repairing and reconditioning the equipment. The college administration should be totally knowledgeable of the procedures developed.

The media program budget provides funds approximating three percent of the total inventory value (replacement cost) of equipment for use in purchasing replacement parts. Authorities recommend that the media program assume the costs of providing replacement lamps, fuses, and similar items.

The director's role in the design and operation of the learning resources center is pivotal. The director must be the person who accepts the prime responsibility for the planning, design and administration of learning resources facilities and programs which can make an important contribution to learning and instruction.

CHAPTER BIBLIOGRAPHY

[1] Baughman, M. Dale, "School Administration: Beatitudes for Beleaguered Bigwigs," Phi Delta Kappan, Vol. 47, No. 6 (February 1966):317-19.

[2] Brown, James W., and Kenneth D. Norberg, Administering Educational Media (New York: McGraw-Hill, 1965).

[3] Diamond, R. M., et. al., Instructional Development for Individualized Learning in Higher Education, Englewood Cliffs, New Jersey: Educational Technology Publications, 1975.

[4] Educational Technology, Individualizing Instruction, Englewood Cliffs, New Jersey: Educational Technology Review Series, 1972.

[5] Erickson, Carlton W. H., Administering Instructional Media Programs, New York: Macmillan Company, 1970.

[6] Finn, James D., "Instructional Technology," Audiovisual Instruction, Vol. 10, No. 3 (March 1965):192-94.

[7] Halpin, Andrew E., Theory and Research in Administration, New York: Macmillan, 1966.

[8] Morphet, Edgar L.; Roe, L. Johns; and Theodore L. Reller, Educational Organization and Administration: Concepts, Practices, and Issues, 2d ed., Englewood Cliffs, New Jersey: Prentice-Hall, 1967.

[9] Torkelson, Gerald M., "Learning Resources," Audiovisual Instruction, Vol. 10, No. 3 (March 1965):199-200.

[10] Woods, Thomas E., The Administration of Educational Innovation (Eugene, Oregon: Bureau of Educational Research, School of Education, University of Oregon, 1967).

CHAPTER V

COMMUNICATION: A CRITICAL FUNCTION IN LEARNING
RESOURCE CENTER MANAGEMENT

Bob Hotes

Several aspects of interpersonal communication as an essential tool for the achievement of effective and efficient administration of learning resources have been considered in preceding chapters. The present chapter discusses some important elements of communication, networks and techniques of communication appropriate to learning resources administration and barriers to effective communication. It also makes some suggestions which may be useful for the development of a personal communications system and strategies by the administrator. Because the assumption is made that effective and efficient administration of learning resources is an important factor in the design and development of effective and efficient learning systems, the function of communication at the administrative level in linking learning resources with faculty teaching methods and techniques and student learning styles will also be considered.

Communication and Management: A Theoretical
Base for Development and Analysis
of Systems for Communicating

As Peter Drucker (13, pp. 4-5) has noted, communication in organizational operations is perception, expectations, and involvement, but communication and information are totally different. Communication involves the coding of information into symbols which can be transmitted, the "sending" or transmission of such symbols, and the reception and interpretation of the symbols by the intended receiver.

On a very broad level, every structured and hierarchical organization may be said to be a system designed for communication, with provision made for flow of information to and from organizational units. If communication is thought of as the sharing of meaning or information between and among individuals, it may be considered a tool through which management in complex organizations is accomplished. Although every organizational chart reveals intended paths of communications flow, however, the actual flow of communication in the management of a complex organization often does not correspond perfectly to the intended pattern. Informal, unplanned communication is often of critical importance to the effective and efficient functioning of an organization. Information transmitted over a cup of coffee in an informal setting may frequently have more impact on individual attidues and opinions than formal memos and reports (27).

Like other functional units within complex organizations, a learning resource center generally can be identified as a component part of a larger communication system. Although a distinction is often made between the kinds of organizational units termed "learning resource centers" and traditional libraries, all operational units whose purpose is to provide access to materials which may aid individuals in learning may be considered learning resource operations. A difficulty arises in the use of the term "learning resources" as a general synonym for nonprint materials such as films, overhead transparencies, slides and video and audiotapes, as contrasted with "hard copy" or printed materials. However, learning resources may be thought to include all media, devices and technologies, as well as the specialized expertise of human resource persons which can be utilized by learners. Under this broad definition, instructional developers and instructional packages may be thought of as learning resources, and the relationship of the administration of learning resources to the instructional programs of schools, colleges, universities and the educational functions of public library systems is clear.

Internal Communications in Learning Resources Administration

The effectiveness of any communication system must be measured by the extent to which that system functions to enable the organization to meet its established objectives and goals. According to some communication theorists, the end product of communication is "isomorphism" or similar structure of meaning achieved in both the senders and the receivers or coded messages (10). Such a level of meaning shared among members of a team provides the basis for effective and efficient operation of the organizational unit.

Accordingly, in the management of internal systems of communication within the organizational structure of a learning resources center or distribution organization, a basis for communication must be established among all members of the operational unit. It is this basis for communication which is a major and critical factor in the effective and efficient operations of the organization. This basis for communication is built upon an understanding by all members of the learning resources organizational team of both broad institutional goals and philosophy and the goals of the learning resources subunit. In other words, a prime task for the administrator of learning resources is to communicate the philosophy and goals of the organization to each member of the learning resources team. Each member of the team must understand the mission of learning resources within the organization and the role which he or she is to play in achieving effective and efficient operation. If the learning resources operation is part of a college or university, for example, each member of the learning resources team must understand what the objectives and goals of the college and university are before he or she can relate the learning resources operation to the institutional mission. Similarly, if a learning resources center is part of a metropolitan library system or attached to a federal, state, or local subunit of government, staff members should understand the philosophy of service under which the particular organization operates in order to relate the learning resources operation to the structure of the whole.

Such a basis of understanding of philosophy, mission, and goals forms the first link in the communication chain within the organization, and its development is an internal communications responsibility of the manager or administrator. The degree of understanding required by each individual team member will naturally vary, depending upon the individual's responsibilities and position in the organizational structure. According to Drucker (13, p. 19), the system of communication established within an organization should start from the intended recipient of communications, rather than from the sender. In Drucker's view, communication which is directed downward in the organizational structure does not work. Downward communication comes only after upward communication has been established. The upward communication must be focused on "something that both recipient and emitter can perceive, focused on something common to both of them," in order to be effective (13, p. 19).

Every member of an organizational team concerned with the management of learning resources at a public community college should have an understanding of how the learning resources concept is related to the conprehensive mission of the college. This knowledge will allow him to ask significant questions regarding his own role in achieving the college mission. Every technician, clerk, secretary and manager should be able to describe learning resources available at the college, and should have at least a general idea of how learning resources available can aid students in learning. At the minimum level, secretaries and clerks should know where to direct students who need help in selecting or utilizing learning resources. If the college subscribes to the philosophical principle that providing maximum opportunities for learning involves making a variety of mediated instructional options, suited to individual student learning styles, available to every student, each member of the learning resources team should be aware of this philosophy and able to communicate pertinent information concerning resources available to students and to others who are interested, including college faculty and staff members and others outside college organization.

The following diagram illustrates, in a simplified form, some aspects of the administrator's role in relating the functions of individual teams members in the learning resources operation to institutional goals through communication. The learning resources manager or administrator serves as a critical link in the chain of communication, relating individual perceptions of organizational philosophy, mission, and goals to actual functions of the learning resources operation. As in all effective processes of communication, feedback from receivers of the messages (staff members, in this case) to the sender (the administrator) is essential.

Elements of Communication:
Techniques and Networks

In an article dealing with the certification and accreditation of educational media personnel, William A. Prigge (32) gives a detailed description and profiles by function of media specialists and technicians in the areas of media management, media product development, and instructional program design. Prigge identifies learning resources management tasks as those functions which have as their purpose the guiding, facilitating, or controlling of

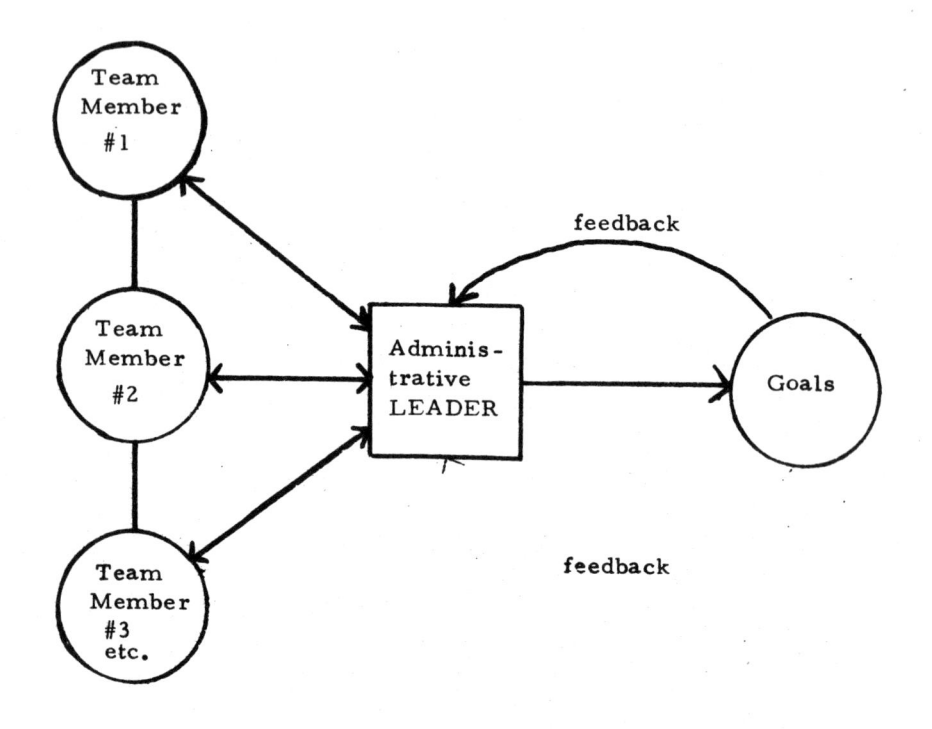

Fig. 1

the learning resources development functions or other learning resources management activities to ensure their effective operation. Each of the functions mentioned by Prigge may be thought to require specific skills in building networks of interpersonal communication in the learning resources organization.

Organization - Management

According to Prigge, the purpose of this function in the context of learning resources operation is to "determine, modify, or execute objectives, philosophy, structure, budget, internal and external relationships and administrative procedures of an organization performing one or several of the LRDFs (Learning Resources Development Functions) or the LRMFs (Learning Resources Management Functions)." Examples of management activities related to this definition include the administration and direction of projects, monitering and changing the operations of the learning resource center, and providing secretarial and maintenance services for the center (32, p. 20).

Each of the aspects of learning resources management noted above implies the use of specific communication skills by the administrator or manager. According to Prigge's formulation, the administration and direction of projects is an activity related to organizational management. Communications competencies appropriate to this function include:

1. The ability to communicate as a leader with those whom the manager or administrator supervises. The administrator must be able to ensure the effective transmission and reception of messages relating to the way in which projects will be carried He or she must be able to establish a network of communication operating within the context of a system of delegated responsibilities and team effort in accomplishing objectives. The administrator must be able to phrase directions and instructions in an acceptable, generally non-threatening form and in language which is clear, concise and as simple as possible. If communication is effective, each member of the project team will be able to answer the questions "What is the expected outcome of this project?" "What is my specific responsibility in bringing this project to completion?" In addition, the administrator must ensure the adequate flow of communication concerning the project in both directions--from his office to the offices and work areas of

all those whom he is directing in the project, and "feedback" communication to him from those whom he supervises. The administrator must also communicate with his own superiors, keeping them informed of progress made in development of the project.

Similarly, in monitoring and changing operations of the learning resources organization, the administrator must depend upon his own ability to communicate in soliciting and interpreting information from those whom he supervises in order to evaluate the present state of organizational operation and to determine the desired direction for change and means which may best accomplish that change. He or she will often have to use every communication skill at his disposal in order to convince other administrators and faculty of the necessity for change.

In determining needs for services and materials which are necessary for the efficient functioning of a learning resources operation, the administrator must be able to communicate with those on the front line of the operation in order to assess needs and to determine how best to meet these needs. The administrator will often find that technical and distribution personnel can provide valuable information on needs for secretarial, clerical and maintenance services. The administrator who is a skillful communicator is able to solicit information and opinions from others without neglecting but actually aiding his responsibility in making decisions.

In particular, the administrator must be able to interpret matters involving operational policy both to superiors and to those whom he supervises, and he must be able to coordinate activities through the effective management of communications flow throughout the structure of the organization, defining and interpreting the content of messages from superiors as well as from the technical and support levels of operation.

2. The ability to select appropriate and effective tools for communicating both within the organization and with individuals who are outside of the organizational structure is a competency essential to learning resources administration.

Selecting Tools or Media for
Internal Communication

Communication within organizations may be classified as formal or informal, organized or unorganized. One of the most important questions facing learning resources administrators with regard to specific communication problems is: In what form and through what means can the individual be reached? The way in which the administrator answers this question will determine the strategy channel and medium chosen to transmit the administrator's message and the form which that message will take.

It is not sufficient for an administrator to be eloquent--although a mastery of clear, concise language is necessary for verbal communication. But an administrator who wishes to communicate successfully with his or her staff, with peers and superiors, and with clients must understand the levels and forms of communication and how to employ them (11, p. 37; 27).

Much of the communication in any organization takes place below the level of conscious control, at the informal level. Formal, structured communication often serves as a reaffirmation or clarification of decisions reached through communication on the informal level (11, p. 39).

In considering individuals for employment or promotion, for example, it not unusual for an administrator or manager to phone a former supervisor of the individual in question, even though a formal recommendation from that same supervisor has been received. The following kind of comment is common in such informal communications:

> "I can't say that Mike's work wasn't satisfactory when he was with our outfit, but, well, you know--he just never seemed to fit in with our way of doing things around here, and, just between you and me . . . ."

Of course, it is still up to the administrator to make the decision on hiring or promotion, but it is no secret that communications on the informal level, like the one noted above, have a powerful influence on administrative practice in many organizations (11, p. 39; 27).

The use of communication on the informal level is legitimate and useful in many circumstances, but special care should be exercised, particularly in the area of employment and promotion, since every aspect of a decision making process may eventually find its way into formal communication. Professor Bob W. Miller, an educator and administrator of broad experience, has noted that communications travel in many directions, and that informal systems of communication may be at least as important as formal systems of communication (27).

The informal level of communication is essential to the operation of all organizations, including the learning resources operation, because there are categories of ideas, instructions and thoughts which may not be acceptable at any other level (11, p. 39). In many cases it would be a mistake, for example, to send a memo concerning an expensive mistake or neglect of professional duty through formal channels until further information has been gained from the parties involved. And sending a report of the adoption of a particular course of action to an individual strongly opposed to that course of action may cause bitterness and serious trouble unless the blow can be softened by informal communication on a personal level (11, p. 39).

Three procedures which can help to give the learning resources administrator a grasp of the elements necessary for effective and efficient informal communication are the following:

1. The administrator should "get out into the field where action is." This contact with individuals on the front line of operation is sometimes called "walking around sense," and it often gives an administrator a chance to contact those in the organization with whom he might not otherwise talk.

2. The administrator should speak the language of those employed in the various aspects of the learning resources operation. Because the learning resources and media fields contain many complex specialties, the administrator must be able to understand and use terms related to a variety of technologies (19). Travers (35, p. 2) has noted that the "audiovisual area" has suffered from the lack of a precise language common to the majority of specialists. Being able to speak the appropriate languages of the technical specialties involved in the learning resources

operation allows the administrator to overcome this barrier to communication, at least in part, and to serve as a communication link between the technical experts in his organizational subunit, administrators in other areas of the parent organization or enterprise, and clients. The learning resources administrator should understand how media can be utilized according to a total systems concept, and he or she should be able to explain this concept to all members of the organization in terms of their own specialties (3).

3. The learning resources administrator must keep up with pertinent developments in technology and will do so by reading, by talking to persons in related fields, by attending conferences and meetings, and by becoming aware of how changes may affect his own learning resources team (11, p. 39).

Forms and Channels of Organized Communication

The fact that the bulk of the communication within an organization normally takes place at an informal level does not mean that systems of formal communication should not be planned and made effective (11, p. 43). Communication will take place whether or not there are forms or recognizable formal channels available, but without formal channels of communication, little control of information flow will be possible. If channels of communication are insufficient at the formal level, informal channels will be overloaded, and individuals within the organization will have difficulty in separating rumors from fact. Without sufficient formal channels of communication, members of an organization cannot secure or control the information necessary to keep the organization functional (11, p. 44).

In addition to the formal contact channels for communication which are described by any institutional or subunit organizational chart there are three major means available to the administrator for use in reaching individuals and groups. These means may be properly considered tools of communication rather than channels of communication because they are flexible and responsive to the needs and purposes of the communicator. These tools are the memorandum and report, business correspondence, and conferences. All three of these forms of communication require the administrator to develop an individual style (11; 27).

Other chapters have dealt with administrative skills which are important in the management of successful conferences. The discussion here will center on ways in which the learning resources administrator can organize conferences as effective tools for establishing communication.

In order to establish and maintain a high level of interpersonal communication among the participants at conferences, the administrator should:

1. Hold conferences on a regularly scheduled basis, so that effective participation can be planned by all involved.
2. Provide each participant with information regarding the purpose, nature, and intended outcomes of the conference.
3. Research issues under consideration and provide appropriate information to all participants.
4. See to it that sufficient discussion takes place to accomplish the purposes of the conference, soliciting participation from reluctant participants when necessary.
5. Express results in a form accessable to all interested parties. Results of the conference may be expressed in the form of minutes, summary reports, etc., and should be disseminated to each participant (11, p. 56).

Some barriers to effective communication through conferences are related to the points listed previously. Lack of foresight in planning for a conference, the failure of the administrator to provide sufficient advance notice for adequate preparation by participants and failure to research the background of issues are all factors which can limit the effectiveness of communication in the conference setting. Personal hostility and animosity among conference participants and inefficient use of time allotted for the conference are additional barriers to effective communication in conferences (27).

Managing Correspondence for Effective Communication

Like many other administrators, the learning resources administrator may find that the volume of correspondence required for the normal conduct of the affairs of the organization has become a serious problem. Miller (27) has referred to the increasing burden of correspondence and paperwork in the daily routines of contemporary administrators as "the paper tiger." The simile is very apt, since paperwork and routine correspondence can devour administrative time and talents if not wisely and efficiently managed.

In general, the key to efficient and effective communication through correspondence is to strive to be clear, concise, and accurate, and to keep constantly in mind what you want to say in the communication and to whom you want to say it.

Following are some techniques which may aid the learning resources administrator in producing correspondence which is effective and efficient as communication.

1. Use printed forms for repetitive correspondence whenever possible and appropriate. Repetitive correspondence may include such items as requests for information concerning various types of media, acknowledgement of inquiries, "feedback" reports on media services and the like.

2. Develop suitable replies for often-asked questions. These may be kept on file for use as guides or models as necessary. Model letters for important correspondence may also be useful. Once a decision as to the appropriate form for a particular kind of correspondence is made, there is little need to go through the same decision making process repeatedly, although forms should be periodically reviewed to make sure that they are up-to-date and still adequate for their intended purpose.

3. Set up a routine or exchange system for copies of important correspondence in order to keep members of the organization informed. This technique will naturally not be appropriate for every type of correspondence.

4. Develop a system of priorities in answering mail.

5. Plan routine correspondence (letters, memoranda, etc.) for a minimum of length consistent with courtesy and warmth.

6. Use personalized memos and notepads instead of dictation when just a few lines are needed.

7. Personalize "form" materials by writing suitable brief comments on them. This technique is not suitable for every kind of correspondence or for every intended receiver (27; 11, pp. 65-68).

Common barriers to communication through correspondence are overcommunication, or circulating an unnecessary amount of written material, and communicating badly or unclearly (11, p. 65). The effective and efficient administrator develops a personalized system for analyzing communications needs and determining whether oral or written communication is most appropriate for the needs of the situation. Proper use of the telephone in administrative communication is another important tool in reducing the burden of correspondence (27).

Reports and Memos

The learning resources administrator will find that memos and reports that are clear, concise and accurate can also be effective and efficient tools for internal communication, if they are part of a planned system of communication developed by the individual administrator. On the other hand, overly complex, wordy and imprecise memos and reports can produce confusion which is a barrier to communication.

De Mare (11, p. 73) suggests three basic criteria for evaluating the effectiveness of a report or memo in communicating:

1. Is the memo or report a useful instrument? What value value does it have for the intended receiver?
2. Does the report or memo indicate the quality of the writer's work? Does it express the character of the writer?
3. Is the report or memo a 'silent salesman' of the writer's authority or competence? In other words, is it persuasive?

In addition, the report or memo should be organized with a title heading and appropriate subheadings so that the reader can identify the parts of the memo or report with minimum effort and maximum accuracy.

External Communication and
Public Relations

Because learning resources management is a client-centered service, the administrator of learning resources will often be concerned with communication relating his or her operation to the total enterprise and to client publics. The publics for each kind of organization and for various kinds or types of communication are unique and individualized (22; 26). A particular subunit in a complex organizational structure may have both external and internal publics, each requiring specialized planning and approaches in a public relations system for communication.

A learning resource center which is an operational subunit within the organizational structure of a comprehensive community college, for example, will have target publics for communication at various levels both within and outside of the organizational structure. Academic administrators, instructors and students may all be considered publics external to the learning resources operation, although they are also parts of the overall structure of the college organization, if the college is thought of as a learning system.

Learning resources administrators will often be concerned with such external communication problems as how to create a favorable image for the learning resources center and its services in the minds of faculty, administrative staff, community and students. Learning resources administrators who are employed by libraries and other public agencies face similar challenges in communicating with administrators and patrons (24).

There are several kinds of tools which can aid the administrator in building systems to communicate with various external publics. These may be classified as media devices designed to convey messages to individuals and groups, and the development of interpersonal communication skills in learning resources staff members through staff development.

Media Devices for Public Communication

The selection of media to establish effective communication involves the determination of the content of the message, the identification of the target audience for communication, and the selection of the appropriate levels of communication or channels. Once the administrator has determined what he desires to communicate to a mass or public audience, the next consideration is an analysis of the nature of that audience. If the intended audience is composed of academic administrators on a particular college campus, for example, an information bulletin with a personal note added by hand might be most effective. If on the other hand, the communication is directed toward students, another medium, a campus poster campaign perhaps, might be the best choice.

In planning for effective and efficient mass or public communication, the learning resources administrator should consult professionals who are experts in the management of public and mass media relations. Colleges, universities and other institutions often have offices responsible for contact with the external public on an official level, the preparation and distribution of news releases and articles, and the organizing of special events. The learning resources administrator should make a serious effort to learn how such offices can aid in planning and developing a favorable image of the learning resources operation (22, p. 19). They can also offer help in selecting the appropriate level or tone for various communications aimed at an external public and aid in relating the communication efforts of the learning resources operation to communications systems and networks of the organization as a whole.

Interpersonal Communication Skills for Learning Resources Staff

Although the selection of appropriate media to convey particular messages to external publics is important, the major factor in the development and maintenance of a favorable public attitude toward the learning resources operation is the level of interpersonal communication possessed by staff members. As previously noted, all members of the learning resources team should be able to deliver appropriate information concerning various aspects of the learning resources operation. However, the way in which such information is delivered is also important. A secretary who does not know how to conduct a polite phone conversation or how to answer questions politely, or a media technician who seems to be surly and morose may build substantial barriers to the process of effective and efficient communication. A major responsibility of the learning resources administrator is to provide necessary education in interpersonal communication skills for staff members and to reinforce correct behavior. The administrator should provide an effective example of how to deal with the public through his or her own behavior.

The learning resources administrator should also be able to serve as a communication channel in relating the activities of the learning resources operation with the teaching and learning styles of individuals. He or she should be aware, for example, of the implications of media selection for cognitive and affective learning, as discussed by Edgar Dale and others (37, pp. 9-12). Knowledge of educational cognitive styles and the functions and implications of such techniques as the mapping of student learning styles will enable the administrator to relate the operations of the learning resources team to the efforts of instructional content specialists in working for the development and improvement of instruction. The knowledge and communication skills of the administrator must often serve as liason between those whose experiences are in the area of technical media production and those whose prime responsibility is in the adaptation of a content field to effective and efficient instructional delivery. As a communicator, the learning resources administrator must be able to direct efforts of individuals with both points of view to the ultimate goal--provision of learning opportunities best suited to the needs of individual clients.

In taking a systems approach to the design and management of communication, the learning resources administrator will not only analyze the communication needs of the components of his or her own organizational subunit, but he or she will also have an overview of the function of communication within the whole organization. Such approach is essential to effective and efficient administration in any institution.

Because the learning resources operation aims at the facilitation of learning, the learning resources administrator often plays a key role in the coordination of instructional development. A principal tool utilized by the administrator in coordinating such efforts at instructional development is a network of communication linking the activities of individuals responsible for the assessment of learner needs and goals and the specification of content with the activities of those who design and produce elements of instructional delivery systems. In establishing and maintaining networks of communication in learning resources development, the administrator must have an operational knowledge of learner cognitive styles as well as a knowledge of instructional styles of individual teachers.

As noted by De Nike and Strother (12, p. 58), recent models developed to provide for the systematic design of instruction reveal a tendency to focus emphasis on learner characteristics as determinants of the emphasis placed on instructional design components. Behaviors used for identifying learner cognitive style may be categorized into three sets: the manner in which a learner gathers information; the manner in which a learner interprets information; and, the manner in which a learner reasons to a decision or conclusion.

The first set of behaviors deals with the kinds of symbols an individual is most proficient at using; that is, whether the learner acquires information from reading words, reading numbers, or listening to words and/or numbers. It also concerns the ability to gather information using any or all of the five senses. The last segment of the set centers on learned social behaviors which enable the learner to get information about persons or experiences (12, p. 58).

The second set of learner behaviors concerns three methods through which the information gathered can be interpreted. Does a person interpret information primarily through contact with his or her peers or through interaction with family and/or other authority groups? Or does he or she usually make independent decisions regarding the meaning of information? And a third set of behaviors focuses on the reasoning processes an individual learner might use to reach a decision on the basis of the information gathered: reasoning through the application of rules, definitions and/or classifications; reasoning through the identification of differences between present and previous information or of similarities between the two sets of data; and reasoning using all three modes (12, p. 58).

Because learner characteristics affect selection of objectives, entry level, depth of treatment, selection of strategies, selection of media, evaluation and revision, there must be a correspondence between learner characteristics and the components of instructional delivery systems (12, p. 59).

In general, the learning resources administrator will approach the problem of determining learner styles from the point of view of a non-specialist. But he or she must be aware of the effects of learning styles in the cognitive affective and psychomotor domains so that he or she can coordinate planning and design of components of instructional delivery systems which will meet particular learner needs.

In addition, the learning resources administrator must be aware of teaching styles as they affect instructional delivery. As an administrator and communicator, he or she will be able to understand various methods of teaching in the classroom as well as ways in which autotutorial and packaged instruction can be utilized so that he or she will be able to coordinate efforts to produce efficient and effective learning materials.

Relationships of classroom instructors to the learning or "information processing" operations of learners have been characterized in many different ways and through the use of many different models (1; 2). The figure which follows on page 92 (fig. 2) is a representation of some of the personal interactions which may take place in a learning setting.

In the model individual students are shown to be linked with an educator system and with each other in efforts to penetrate the field of study. Not all students make contact with or penetrate the field of study at the point of focus of the educator system. As illustrated in figure two, some learners ($S_{5(b)}$ for example) have minimal direct contact with the educator system, which includes the teacher and other instructional delivery elements, such as instructional packages.

As described in the categories of learning behaviors listed by De Nike and Strother (12, p. 58), peer contact may be the most important element in the learning styles of such students.

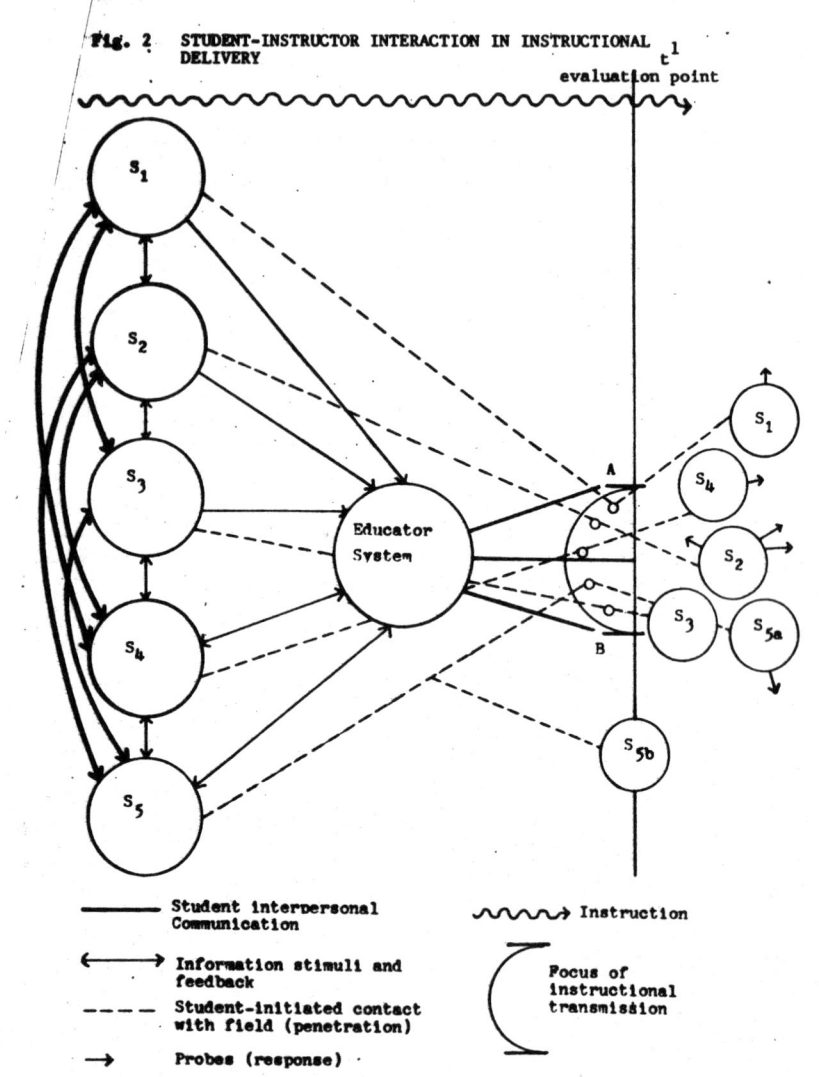

Fig. 2 STUDENT-INSTRUCTOR INTERACTION IN INSTRUCTIONAL DELIVERY

t^1 evaluation point

— Student interpersonal Communication
⟵⟶ Information stimuli and feedback
- - - - Student-initiated contact with field (penetration)
⟶ Probes (response)
⁓⁓⟶ Instruction
) Focus of instructional transmission

Functioning as a communication link, the learning resources administrator can develop and maintain a network of communication to focus all efforts of the members of his or her team on the development of resources suited to learning styles and needs. Unless communication and coordination among all elements involved in the design and delivery of instruction is achieved and amintained, efforts to improve instruction will often fail (16, pp. 28-29).

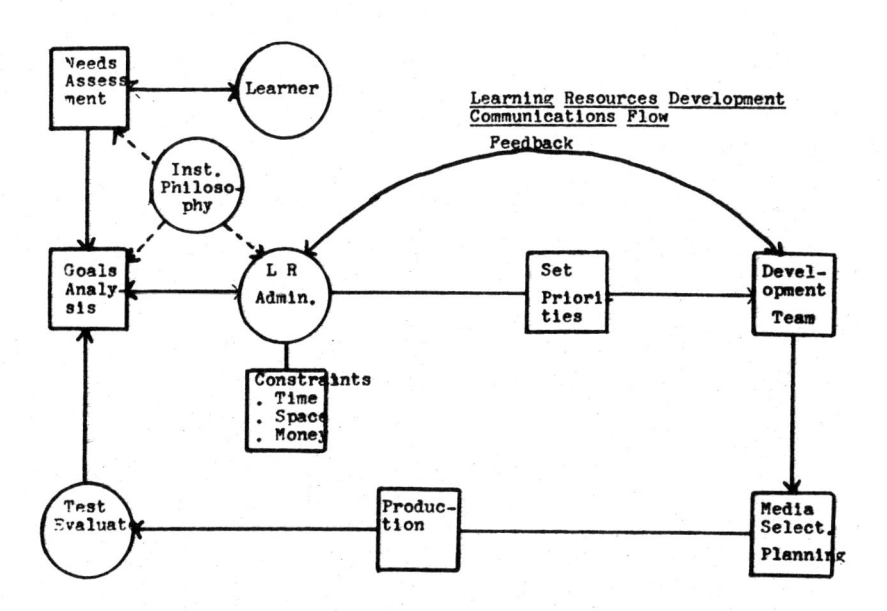

Fig. 3

CHAPTER BIBLIOGRAPHY

[1] Briggs, Leslie J., "The Teacher and Programmed Instruction: Roles and Role Potentials," Audiovisual Instruction 2 (May 1964):273-76.

[2] Brown, R. W. Bill, "Computorized, Objectives-Based Media Selection," Educational Technology 15 (November 1975):57.

[3] Bynon, Robert, "The Total Systems Concept, Research Implications," Instructional Technology, Frederick G. Knirk and John C. Childs, editors, New York, Holt, Rinehart and Winston, 1968.

[4] Cason, Gerald J., "The Information Processing Approach: Organizing Instructional Content," Educational Technology 15 (October 1975):21-25.

[5] Chambers, David W., "Educational Technology Research: Putting Down the Discovery Learning Hypothesis," Educational Technology 11 (March 1971):54-59.

[6] Chapman, Dave, and Frank Carioti, Design for ETV: Planning for Schools with Television, Chicago, Chapman Design, Inc., 1968.

[7] Childs, John E., "The Effect of an Open Mind on School Innovation," Instructional Technology, Frederick G. Knirk and John W. Childs, editors, New York, Holt Rinehart and Winston, 1968.

[8] Clegg, Janet, and Michael R. Simonson, "A Review of Educational Media Research: The Sex Variable," AV Communication Review 23 (Winter 1975):427-31.

[9] Darrow, Richard W., Dan F. Forrestal and Aubrey O. Cookman, The Dartnell Public Relations Handbook, Chicago, Dartnell Corporation, 1967.

[10] De Fleur, Melvin, Theories of Mass Communication, New York, David McKay Company, Inc., 1966.

[11] De Mare, George, Communicating for Leadership, New York, Ronald Press Company, 1968.

[12] De Nike, Lee, and Seldon D. Strother, "A Learner Characteristic Vital to Instructional Development: Educational Cognitive Style," Educational Technology 15 (September 1975): 58-59.

[13] Drucker, Peter F., Technology, Management and Society, New York, Harper and Row, 1967.

[14] Faesler, Len, and Phillip T. West, "The Media Administrator: Instructional Leader of the Future?" Educational Technology 15 (July 1975):43-45.

[15] Fessler, Ralph, "A Model for School-Community Relations," Educational Technology 15 (November 1975):52-56.

[16] Harris, Clifton S., Jr., and Ralph C. Atkinson, Jr., "A Grand Experiment in Media-Supported Instruction: What Went Wrong," Educational Technology 15 (January 1976): 23-29.

[17] Heinich, Robert, "The Teacher in an Instructional System," Instructional Technology, Frederick G. Knirk and John W. Childs, editors, New York, Holt, Rinehart and Winston, 1968, pp. 45-60.

[18] Houle, Cyril O., The Design of Education, San Francisco, Jossey-Bass Publishers, 1972.

[19] Howe, Harold, II, "Education and the Changing Technology," Education . . . Everybody's Business, Washington, D.C., United States Government Printing Office, 1967, pp. 17-23.

[20] Jernstedt, Christian G., "The Relative Effectiveness of Individualized and Traditional Instruction Methods," Journal of Educational Research 69 (February 1976):211-18.

[21] Keegan, John J., "Performance-Based Staff Evaluation: A Reality We Must Face," Educational Technology 15 (November 1975):35-38.

[22] Kobre, Sidney, Successful Public Relations for Colleges and Universities, New York, Hastings House, 1974.

[23] Kumata, Hideya, "Two Studies in Classroom Teaching by Television," The Impact of Educational Television, Urbana, University of Illinois Press, 1960, pp. 151-92.

[24] Loizeaux, Marie D., Publicity Primer, New York, H. W. Wilson Co., 1959.

[25] Lumsdaine, Arthur A., "An Evaluation of Programmed Instruction Today," Instructional Technology, Frederick G. Knirk and John W. Childs, editors, New York, Holt, Rinehart and Winston, 1968, pp. 75-80.

[26] McCloskey, Gordon, Education and Public Understanding, New York, Harper and Row, 1954.

[27] Miller, Bob W., unpublished notes, North Texas State University, Denton, Texas 1976.

[28] Moore, Omar Khayam, "From Tools to Interactional Machines," Instructional Technology, Frederick G. Knirk and John G. Childs, editors, New York, Holt, Rinehart and Winston, 1968, pp. 99-105.

[29] O'Banion, Terry, Teachers for Tomorrow, Tucson, University of Arizona Press, 1973.

[30] Phillips, Murray G., "Learning Materials and Their Implementations," Review of Educational Research 26 (June 1966):373-79.

[31] Pilnick, Carl, and Harry R. Glixon, A Primer on Telecommunications in Education, Washington, D.C., Synergetics, Inc., 1972.

[32] Prigge, William C., "Certification and Accreditation of Educational Media Personnel: A Frame of Reference," Audiovisual Instruction 18 (May 1973):16-20.

[33] Savage, Arthur L., "Increasing Empathetic Capabilities of Instructional Developers: Evaluation of a Three-Phase Instructional Strategy," AV Communication Review 23 (Winter 1975):415-26.

[34] Schram, Wilbur, "What We Know About Learning from Instructional Television," Educational Television: The Next Ten Years, Wilbur Schram, editor, Stanford, Institute for Communications Research, 1962, pp. 52-71.

[35] Travers, Robert M. W., Man's Information System, Scranton, Pa., Chandler Publishing Co., 1970.

[36] _____, "The Transmission of Information to Human Receivers," AV Communications Review 12 (September 1964): 373-85.

[37] Wager, Walter, "Media Selection in the Affective Domain: A Further Interpretation of Dale's Cone of Experience for Cognitive and Effective Learning," Educational Technology 15 (July 1975):9-13.

[38] Wallace, Sarah Leslie, and associates, Patrons Are People, Chicago, American Library Association, 1956.

[39] Weiner, Richard, Professional's Guide to Public Relations Services, Englewood Cliffs, N.J., Prentice-Hall, Inc., 1968.

CHAPTER VI

LEARNING RESOURCES AND INSTRUCTIONAL
DEVELOPMENT

Aylene Hegar

The topic of instructional development is becoming more and more prevalent each year at all levels of public and private education and more particularly in the field of higher education. Gustafson notes the following indications of increasing adoption of instructional development practices throughout the country:

1. A survey of a limited sample of higher education institutions by Lee indicates that considerable instructional development is being conducted at that level; and at the public school level, interest is indicated by the large number of requests for Instructional Development Institutes.

2. A significant increase in membership in the Division for Instructional Development of the Association for Educational Communications and Technology is another indicator of heightened interest (3, pp. 122-23).

Definition of Instructional Development

There is yet no agreed upon definition of instructional development that is mutually satisfactory to its practitioners. A series of papers published by the Division for Instructional Development (DID) at the Association for Educational Communications (AECT) presents five somewhat varying views of what instructional development is. It is significant that each paper was prepared by an Instructional Developer (3, pp. 121-22).

The most encompassing definition of instrudtional development would seem to be any organized effort by one instructor or a team of individuals to improve the quality of instruction. Berchin refers to I.D. as the total process of developing instruction rather than dealing with isolated components such as media, instrudtional objectives, etc. Systematic rather than cosmetic changes in instruction are emphasized by Diamond. Carmichael, as a practitioner and implementer, defines I.D. as "A systematic (logical) process for improving instruction and student learning"

(4, p. 371). When we are talking about systematic instructional design says Mager, we are talking about sensible design, about "thinking in the whole" rather than about "thinking in isolated pieces" (1, Foreward).

Processes Involved in Instructional Development

Despite the lack of any precise definition of instru tional development, it can be said that, in general, its practitioners do agree that it includes at least the following processes: (1) problem definition; (2) design and production of one or more means of solving a problem; (3) evaluation of results; and, (4) revision, if required (3, p. 122).

Some broad functions of I. D. have been indicated from the models of Briggs, Brown, Baker and Schutz, Davies and Farris. They are:

1. Task Analysis--determining what is to be learned.

2. Specifying Objectives--stating what needs to be learned in a measurable way.

3. Learner Analysis--assessing the learners' performance level, learning style, learning rate, self-image, etc.

4. Instruction--providing effective and efficient instruction.

5. Evaluation--determining if the learning program is successfully realizing the learning objectives.

6. Motivation--encouraging, leading, and inspiring students to realize the learning objectives.

7. Management--making sure all functions are being performed effectively, efficiently and in proper order (4, p. 267).

Instructional Development Models

Choosing a model to fit a particular educational situation depends upon the audience being addressed and the requirements of the learning situation. Two models are discussed and illustrated in this chapter. The reader is invited to further explore additional models by reading ERIC document ED 059629, "The Systematic Development of Instruction: An Overview and Basic Guide to the Literature," by Paul A. Twelker and others.

Bruce W. Tuckman and Keith J. Edwards propose a systems model for the development and management of instruction. The model is broken down into three phases:

1. Analysis, which includes (a) specification of post-instruction tasks (b) restatement of task as behavioral objectives (c) specification of a sequence of behavioral objectives.

2. Synthesis, which involves two activities occurring in parallel (a) specification of instructional activities and (b) design of evaluative procedures.

3. Operation which includes two simultaneous activities (a) carrying out the instructional activities and the collection of evaluative data.

Following these three phases comes the fourth activity, feedback and iteration, wherein the data collected during the phase of operation are fed into the system so that it can be tested, validated and redesigned based on input data (9, p. 21). See figure 1 for an illustration of this model.

According to Davies, designing a learning system or program involves an orderly sequence of fifteen (15) activities. These are summarized in figure 2. The fifteen activities can be organized under the headings of:

1. Planning.--This involves activities 1, 2, 3, 4, 5, 6, 14, and 15. All of these are concerned with defining the real nature of the problem that the learning system has to overcome.

2. Organizing.--Activities 7 and 11 are involved here. Organizing pertains to the arrangement of learning and teaching resources to accomplish the agreed upon plans.

3. Leading.--This is the way in which the teacher adds himself to the system so as to guide, help, and inspire his students. Activities 8 and 9 are involved here.

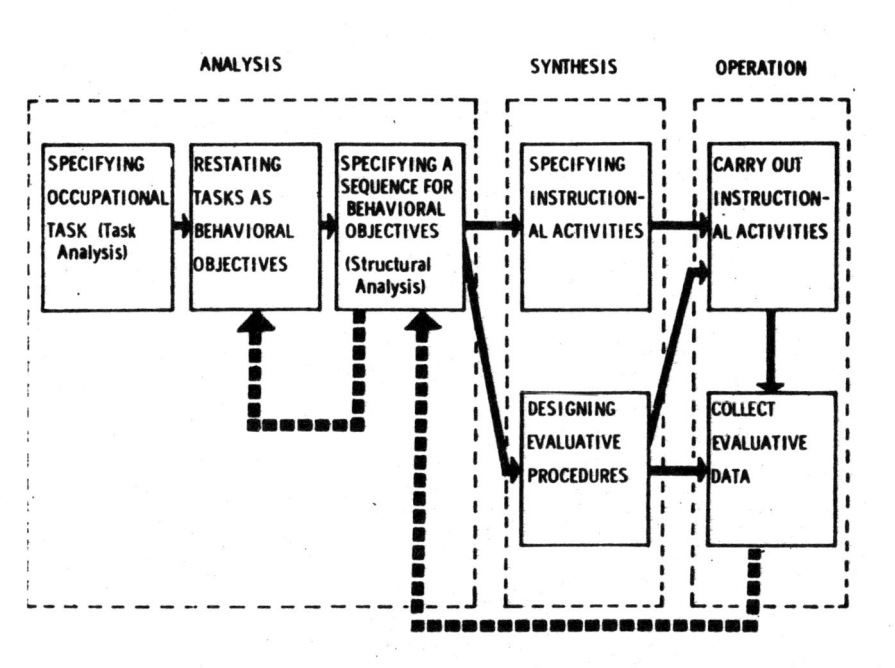

Fig. 1

(9, p. 21)

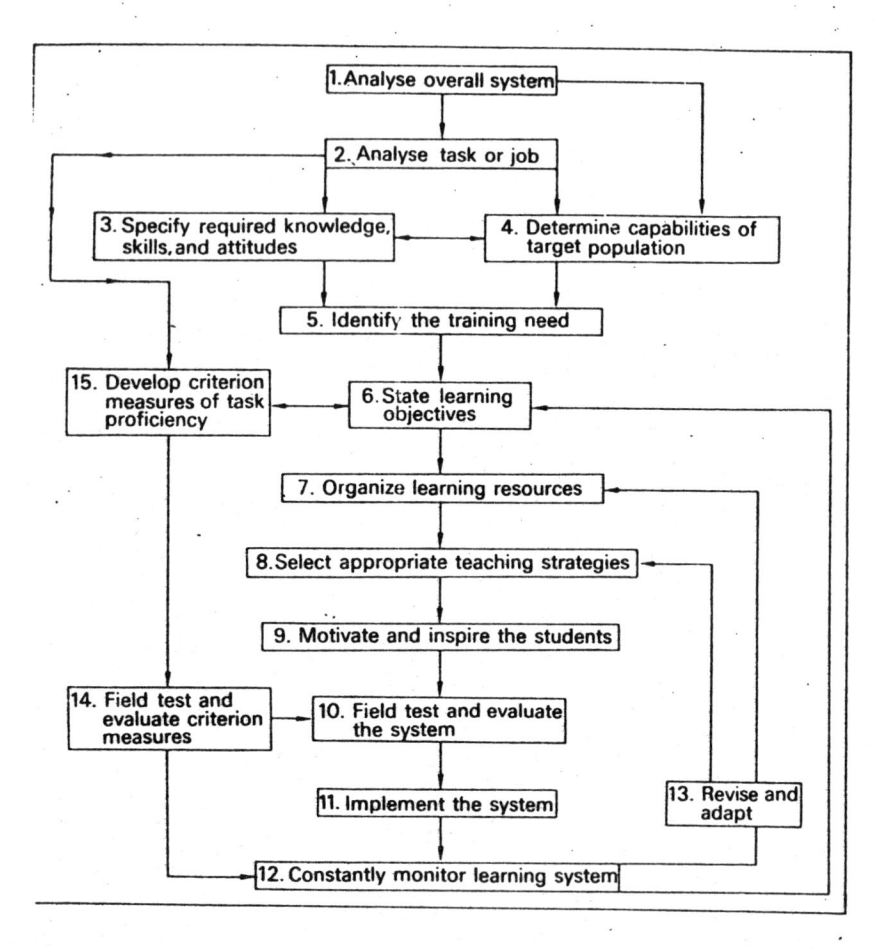

Fig. 2

4. Controlling.--This deals with the evaluation of the success of the learning system. Activities 10, 12, and 13 are involved here.

Staff Organizational Models for Managing I. D.

The instructional development team approach of combining different personnel with varying levels of expertise and responsibility is just beginning to emerge. A variety of persons are engaged in instructional development tasks and in various settings. In one situation a person may play all roles. In another, a project leader may work with a number of specialists (i.e. media, evaluation, curriculum, etc.) and a learning psychologist to develop an instructional product (3, p. 124).

The range of the number and variety of people involved in various levels of instructional development presupposes organization and management of such activities.

According to Knirk and Ware, any management problem relating to I. D. whether it be designing instructional materials to meet behavioral objectives, creating and managing a system for their distribution and use, guiding personnel in instructional or production responsibilities, planning broad programs to meet educational needs, or selecting appropriate areas for research and designing ways to explore them--all require the same broad plan of action (6, p. 42). This plan can be organized under four basic steps:

1. Planning
2. Directing
3. Leading
4. Controlling

Although most educational institutions utilize these four steps to accomplish educational tasks, every educational institution has a different organizational structure. This is primarily due to the fact that structures are largely determined by human factors such as (1) personalities (2) administrative interests (3) financial considerations (4) size and type of institution and (5) physical facilities (4, p. 371).

Two ways of organizing are discussed by Carmichael. One way is to have the instructional development staff report directly to the top administration. One disadvantage to this plan is that faculty members may shy away from top administrators, especially when "evaluation" is part of the situation (10, p. 3). The organizational approach preferred by Carmichael is to have the heads of technical services, public services, production services and instructional development be responsible to an associate dean in charge of the learning resources center. See figure 3.

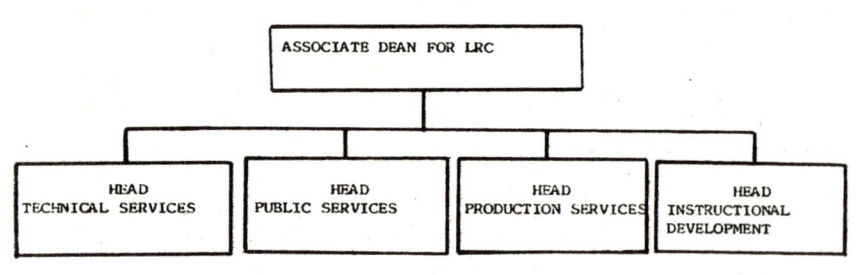

```
                    ┌─────────────────────────┐
                    │ ASSOCIATE DEAN FOR LRC  │
                    └────────────┬────────────┘
          ┌──────────────┬───────┴───────┬──────────────┐
    ┌─────┴─────┐  ┌─────┴─────┐  ┌──────┴──────┐  ┌────┴─────┐
    │   HEAD    │  │   HEAD    │  │    HEAD     │  │   HEAD   │
    │ TECHNICAL │  │  PUBLIC   │  │ PRODUCTION  │  │INSTRUCT. │
    │ SERVICES  │  │ SERVICES  │  │  SERVICES   │  │DEVELOPMT.│
    └───────────┘  └───────────┘  └─────────────┘  └──────────┘
```

Fig. 3

In organizing to accomplish development in a better way, Lane Community College has changed from a former fairly traditional pattern consisting of an Office of Instruction headed by the Dean of Instruction, an Office of the Dean of Students and the Office of the Business Manager to a structure divided along functional lines. The organization now has an Office of Instructional Operations, an Office of Student Services and an Office of Business Operations. The top part of the former jobs were interfaced into the new Office of Academic and College Planning. The new structure allows the deans to have responsibility all the way across the college with regard to planning and development (4, p. 104). See figure 4.

The reader is referred to Holloway's monographs entitled Implementing Instructional Development Through Learning

DIVISION OF ASSIGNED AUTHORITY

PLANNING

⬇

PERSONNEL
EVALUATION

| AUTHORITY AND RESPONSIBILITY ASSIGNED BY THE PRESIDENT |

FORMER PATTERN

PLANNING

⬇

PERSONNEL
EVALUATION

| OFFICE DEAN OF INSTRUCTION | OFFICE DEAN OF STUDENTS | OFFICE BUSINESS MANAGER |

REVISED PATTERN

PLANNING

⬇

PERSONNEL
EVALUATION

| OFFICE ACADEMIC AND COLLEGE PLANNING |||
| OFFICE INSTRUCTIONAL OPERATIONS | OFFICE STUDENT SERVICES | OFFICE BUSINESS OPERATIONS |

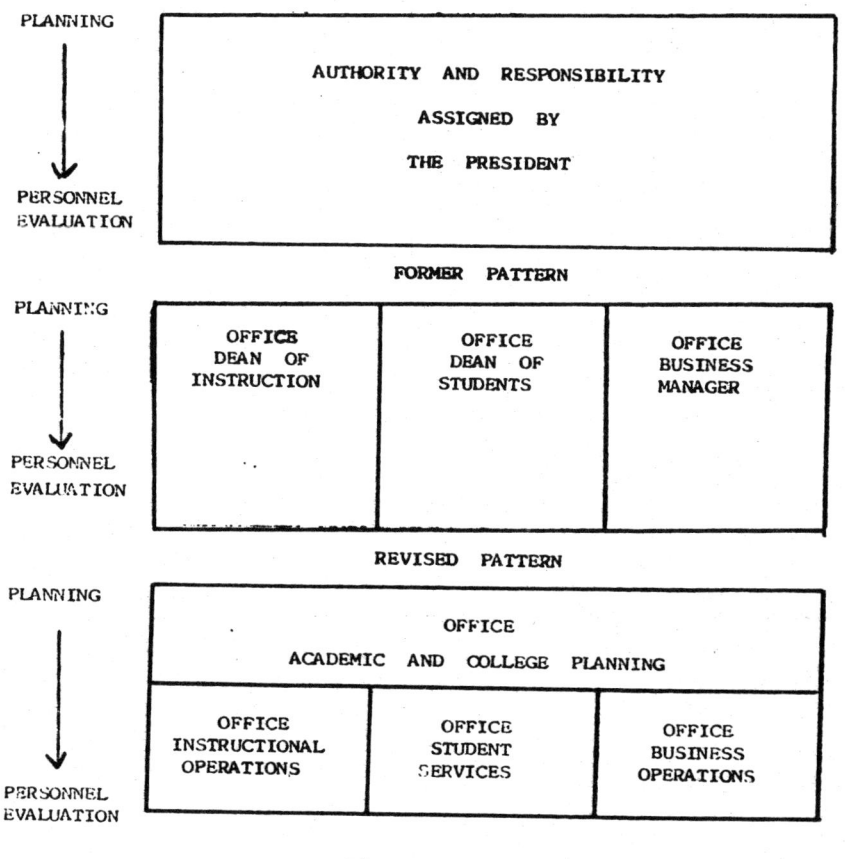

Fig. 4

(5, p. 104)

Resource Programs, Volumes I and II, for a comprehensive listing and discussion of community college staff organizational charts.

Implementing Instructional Development

Instructional development models may be viewed as road maps to writing instruction. Staff organizational models are means of arranging resources to accomplish objectives. They increase stability by reducing uncertainty about what is to be done (1, p. 9). However, in the utilization of these models several important elements are to be considered. Getting faculty interest, effectively involving and rewarding them is crucial. The instructional developer administrator may use a variety of ways to accomplish this. Among them are:

1. Helping instructors analyse how they can best use their time through effective planning.
2. Communicating appropriately what the instructional developer can offer.
3. Providing instructional development funds for faculty instructional projects.
4. Rewarding through released time, money, letters of recognition, etc.
5. Seeking out faculty through appropriate means but not going to them with a superior attitude.
6. Helping faculty build self-confidence and feel secure in writing instruction.

Conclusion

Instructional development, although in its embryonic stage, has exhibited considerable vitality and vigor in the educational scene. It is still searching for its identity and must necessarily concern itself with maturing. It should continue to use its processes critically, continually evaluating and improving methodology and practice.

* * *

NOTE: Due to page-size limitations, several of the diagrams in this chapter are not reproduced in full.

CHAPTER BIBLIOGRAPHY

[1] Davies, Ivor K., Competency Based Learning: Technology, Management, and Design, New York, St. Louis, San Francisco, McGraw-Hill Book Company, 1971.

[2] Drucker, Peter F., The Effective Executive, New York, Evanston, and London, Harper & Row Publishers, 1966.

[3] Gustafson, Kent L., "Instructional Development: The State of the Art," Educational Media Yearbook, 1973, New York and London, R. R. Bowker Company, 1973.

[4] Holloway, Ralph, ed., Implementing Instructional Development Through Learning Resources Programs, Vol. I, Mesquite, Texas, Eastfield College, 1975.

[5] Holloway, Ralph, ed., Implementing Instructional Development Through Learning Resources Programs, Vol. II, Mesquite, Texas, Eastfield College, 1975.

[6] Knirk, Frederick and Mary C. Ware, "The Tools of Instructional Technology," Educational Technology, Vol. XIII, No. 12 (December 1972), 41-42.

[7] Maughn, Lee A., "A Survey of Instructional Development Programs in Higher Education," Audiovisual Instruction, Vol. 17, No. 8 (October 1972), 16-17.

[8] Popham, W. James and Grant R. Cary, Bruce Chilstrom, Ants L. Leps, Thomas M. Miller, and Robert Saxe, "Performance Tests for Instructional Developers: An Exploratory Investigation," Educational Technology, Vol. XIV, No. 3 (March 1974), 57-61.

[9] Tuckerman, Bruce W. and Keith J. Edwards, "A Systems Model for Instructional Design and Management," Educational Technology, Vol. XI, No. 9 (September 1971), 21-26.

[10] Voegel, George H., ed., Using Instructional Technology, San Francisco, Washington and London, Jossey-Bass, Inc., 1975, 3-7.

CHAPTER VII

SERVICES AND MATERIALS PROVIDED THROUGH
A LEARNING RESOURCE CENTER

Kenneth Roach

Of equal importance with the provision of appropriate learning spaces and a suitable learning environment in the learning resources center (LRC) is the careful selection and production of learning materials. The evolution of the provision of services and materials in the LRC has been a process of unfolding, development, growth, and change. Simplistic forms, techniques, and patterns have become more diverse and complex as well as more meaningful to their role as one of the most dynamic elements of American higher education.

Perhaps the most important document yet produced relating to LRC programs is the Guidelines for Two-Year College Learning Resources Programs jointly produced and published by the American Library Association (ALA), The American Association for Educational Communications and Technology (AECT). In defining the role of LRCs and their direct relationships to institutional and instructional objectives, the guidelines isolate four major roles:

> 1. To provide leadership and assistance in the development of instructional systems which employ effective and efficient means of accomplishing those objectives; 2. to provide an organized and readily accessible collection of materials and supportive equipment needed to meet institutional, instructional, and individual needs of students and faculty; 3. to provide a staff qualified, concerned and involved in serving the needs of students, faculty, and community; 4. to encourage innovation, learning, and community service by providing facilities and resources which will make them possible. (3, p. 52)

Based on the stated mission of the college and their written objectives, LRCs offer a variety of services to faculty members and students including consultation, selection of materials, cataloging, scheduling, development, production, distribution and maintenance.

Consultation

Consultative services offered to faculty members range in scope from traditional library reference work to staff and instructional development programs. Traditional library functions serving the faculty make available through resources of professional collections information about recent developments in learning theory, curricular subject areas and education in general. Specific reference services to individual faculty members include bibliographic searches, location of materials for faculty research projects, and interlibrary loan services.

As a support to the teaching process of an educational institution, many LRC programs have extended their services beyond traditional library and media resources to offer consultation in instructional development, curriculum planning, designing instructional experiences, and use of innovative instructional methods. With instructional resources consultants, materials specialists, librarians, media specialists, and instructional developers working in concert with one another, the LRC is uniquely able to assist in all areas of instructional analysis and improvement.

Faculty development programs of in-service training to increase knowledge of the learning processes, effective use of educational technology and the improvement of learning through traditional and innovative uses of library and media resources and services are strengthening faculties and enabling them to become and remain leaders in the field of higher education. As a liaison between administration, faculty, professional organizations and students, the LRC is able to furnish the latest educational information to all concerned with the teaching and learning processes (4).

Selection

In order to provide an organized and readily accessible collection of materials to meet institutional, instructional, and individual needs of students and faculty, the learning resources programs must develop strong capabilities in the area of collection development. Materials should be selected and acquired or designed and produced on the basis of institutional goals and instructional objectives. To accomplish these things a written selection policy must be developed with the aid of all segments of the academic community to reflect criteria that will insure the acquisition of needed materials both book and non-book. An example of a written selection policy and supportive documents are included in the appendix of this book.

The guidelines for LRCs specifically designate the following areas of collection development as important:

Representative works of high caliber which might arouse intellectual curiosity, counteract parochialism, help to develop critical thinking and cultural appreciation, or stimulate use of the resources for continuing education and personal development are included in the collection even though they do not presently meet direct curricular needs.

Materials reflect ages, cultural backgrounds, intellectual levels, developmental needs, and vocational goals represented in the student body.

The reference collection includes a wide selection of significant subject and general bibliographies, authoritative lists, periodical indexes, and standard reference works in all fields of knowledge.

Newspapers with various geographical, political and social points of view on national and state issues are represented in the collection.

Government documents are required as significant sources of information.

Files of pamphlets and other ephemeral materials are maintained.

The conservation of materials, as well as the elimination of those which are obsolete, should be developed as part of on-going procedures.

The Learning Resources Unit functions as an archive for historical information and documents concerning the college itself.

Responsibility for the collection and preservation of community history and for the accumulation of other local and statistical data is shared with other institutions and is coordinated with them. (3, pp. 60-61)

It is important that curricular materials and all other areas mentioned in the guidelines provide materials presenting all sides of controversial issues. Rationale for this professional position are given by the American Library Association and other related associations concerned with censorship and the free communication of information. All board members, administrators, faculty, and LRC staff members should be familiar with these positions and support them with written documents.

Collection development is concerned with books, non-book materials, and the production of materials. Building the quality book collection is a difficult and time consuming responsibility which rests mainly with the LRC library staff. Successful acquisition rests upon the processes employed and the involvement of college personnel and students. To promote this involvement there are certain elements that must be incorporated in the selection process.

1. A clear understanding of what kind of library the college is supposed to be building and for what kinds of users; 2. a genuine and general awareness of the different roles which different books . . . play in the intellectual life of those who come to . . . the library; 3. an effective organization for involving the faculty and library staff in book selection; and 4. a liberal and assured annual fund with regular annual increases for book purchases. (29, p. 40)

Generally speaking, the book collection of an academic library should contain materials in several broad areas: books supporting the curriculum of the college, a professional collection for faculty use, recreational reading, and selective and representative reference books. The variety, breadth, and depth of collection in these areas will be dictated by institutional goals, budgetary restrictions, selection policies, and review and selection personnel.

Although these guidelines for LRCs are qualitative in nature, quantity also is a consideration in meeting student and faculty needs; therefore, a quantitative supplement is not being prepared which will add this dimension in assessing the adequacy of the learning resources program. Other elements which affect the development of the academic library quantitatively as well as qualitatively are proximity of other library collections, interlibrary loan programs and other cooperative library arrangements, size of student body and instructional staff, and faculty commitment to assignments which stimulate library use (18, pp. 16-17).

Many selection aids are available to library and instructional staff for the careful consideration of materials to be added to the book collection. Most professional journals in every discipline contain reviews of current books and materials being published in that subject area. These journals will be available either in the library or through personal subscriptions held by individual faculty members. Other professional review periodicals which are part of any academic working collection include Library Journal, the New York Times Book Review, and Choice, a monthly periodical which contains reviews of academic books written by subject specialists and giving level of intended use. Many other periodical selection aids are available to strengthen collections. Other selection aids and bibliographies of standard books useful in academic libraries include: The Junior College Library Collection, Books for College Libraries, Books for Junior Colleges, A Basic Book Collection for the Community College, and The Vocational Technical Library Collection. Special subject lists are published by professional associations and other groups to form standard core lists from which to order or against which to check to fill in gaps in collections (7, pp. 44-64).

Although selection criteria for content is the same, selection procedures and considerations for audiovisual materials present other problems which should be considered in the selection process before acquisition. In a very pronounced way, commercially produced media software is affected by market trends. Many firms release and promote products dealing with topics which they feel will be in demand. The selector's problem then becomes separating the worthwhile from the hastily produced material. An additional problem is that nonprint reviews are far less developed than those for books. Many reviews are descriptive, not evaluative and much material is reviewed late or not at all (24, p. 113). Previews is a journal which publishes reviews and

TITLE
THEY'RE PUBLISHING A THOUSAND NEW BOOK TITLES A DAY, THANK GOODNESS, I DON'T HAVE TO READ THEM!

announcements for forthcoming media for all types of libraries. The national Information Center for Educational Media has published several indexes covering various formats. Other review materials are found in The Media Review Digest supplement found in monthly issues of Audiovisual Instruction and published annually in the Media Review Index. This index includes reviews from over thirty journals which review audiovisual instructional materials.

In addition to the selection criteria demanded of book material, nonprint materials must meet technical excellence standards in many areas. In the selection process questions which must be answered are:

1. Is technical quality of the material artistic?
2. Is the producer's mode of communication adequate for the purpose? That is, is the message put over clearly, forcefully, in ways that attract and hold attention?
3. Are physical size, format, and color satisfactory?
4. Is workmanship in the construction of the material adequate?
5. Is the content to be presented free of conflicts and distractions?
6. Was careful planning by the producer obvious in the content structure of the material?
7. Did the producer of the material set out to produce the material for school audiences with competent educational consultants? (15, pp. 328-29)

Because of their greater expense, wider audience distribution, and lack of appropriate reviews, nonprint materials are still best selected by actual preview. Several constraints limit the effectiveness of a preview program for the selection of non print materials: Facilities and equipment must be dedicated to preview programs; many producers refuse to furnish preview copies of materials or charge a fee for such services; and the lack of staff time for this very time consuming procedure. Current practices vary widely in conducting preview programs, but this procedure for the selection of a quality nonprint collection should not be overlooked (38). Basic lists of selected mediagraphic sources are available in a variety of published and unpublished materials and should be consulted in establishing selection procedures (12).

Necessary in the consideration of the selection of nonprint materials is the evaluation and selection of hardware with which to use the software. General criteria for the selection of hardware should include the following: portability, ruggedness, cost, ease of operation, quality of performance, effective design, ease of maintenance and repair, reputation of the manufacturer, local equipment status and available services (7, p. 63).

Designated objectives for the use of the hardware should be determined before the evaluation and selection process begins. Selection should be made in reference to the criteria set forth above and with the idea of standardization to yield the following advantages:

1. It is easier to train teachers and students to operate the equipment; hence less time and effort will be spent by supervisory personnel on this phase of service.
2. There will be fewer operational failures in the classroom because more people will understand how to control the output of the equipment.
3. It is easier to service one make of machine because local servicemen are more familiar with it and understand how to fix or adjust it.
4. It is cheaper to service the equipment, since only one set of spare parts needs to be maintained. Therefore, less money needs to be tied up in a stock of spare parts during any one year.
5. There is less clerical and technical work involved in maintaining the inventory of spare parts, and in storing, organizing, and finding space for them.
6. Standardization under school system policy eliminates wrangling with distributors every time an order is sent out for bids. (15, p. 100)

Successful selection of books, nonprint materials and equipment will determine the success and utilization of the materials located in the LRC. Collection development is a slow process and success depends on a long history of carefully developed selection processes, coupled with close faculty-library cooperation designed to meet the instructional and institutional objectives of the college.

Cataloging

The rationale for cataloging and classifying material, book and nonbook, in an LRC continues to be the making the material as accessible as possible to faculty and students. Many decisions for the organization of materials in the LRC must be made and one of the most important is that for the classification and cataloging of materials. User needs must be constantly analyzed to determine if the interpretation of book and nonbook collections is meeting the bibliographic and location needs of LRC patrons. It is imperative that materials be organized in such a way that all, not just some or most of them, are readily available and useful to those who need them (15, p. 107). Historically, because of the absence of any standardized method or tools for organizing collections of nonprint materials, many were faced with the task of developing their own methods of dealing with the problem. More recently national associations (6), and others (23; 20) have developed guidelines and codes for handling problems associated with nonbook mediagraphic control. With the recent publication of the revised chapter 12 of the Anglo-American Cataloging Rules, it is to be hoped that bibliographic control of nonbook materials is well on its way to being an established fact.

Cataloging is the attempt on the part of libraries and media collections to communicate with the patron. The introduction to the Anglo-American Cataloging Rules indicated that "a coherent code of cataloging rules requires a fundamental orientation in respect to the type of library, the type of collection, and the type of catalog for which it is designed" (2, p. 1). This statement could be further expanded to include the type of user for which the cataloging is being developed.

Book cataloging and classification has a long history of development culminating in the Anglo-American Cataloging Rules published jointly by The American Library Association, The Library of Congress, The Library Association and the Canadian Library Association published in 1967 and again in 1970. Because of the inadequacy of earlier work, several separately published chapters have been recently published for nonbook material. Cataloging rules for microforms are included in a separately published chapter six released in 1974, recently chapter 12 was revised in a separately published monograph for audiovisual media and special instructional materials, and in 1977 a revision of rules for the cataloging of sound recordings will be issued.

Closely associated with cataloging of book and nonbook materials is the question of classification systems. The Dewey Decimal Classification and the Library of Congress Classification systems are the two major systems used in this country and recent studies indicate that time has done little to satisfy questions about which system should be selected for use by small or medium sized academic libraries. Recent trends have shown preference for the LC system especially among new collections and larger academic collections.

To conserve staff, effort and money, many libraries are entering into cooperative cataloging systems on a district basis or on a national basis with systems like the Ohio College Library Center (OCLC). The OCLC system connected by direct computer terminal to each of its member libraries greatly aids in the cataloging process by producing catalog cards by computer upon demand. Cards are produced for each library according to their prescribed needs and are immediately sent to the ordering library. Plans are for nonbook cataloging capabilities to be added soon to OCLC computers thus making the service more tailored to the needs of LRCs than has previously been possible. Time saved through cooperative cataloging allows material to be quickly processed and shelved for more immediate use by LRC patrons.

Production

Administration of production services must include developing appropriate policies, establishing production controls and procedures, developing specifications and contracts for production performed by commercial firms, and giving proper attention to copyrights and permissions of published materials (10, pp. 251-73).

The most distinctive feature of LRC programs is the acceptance of the responsibility to produce instructional materials that do not exist commercially. Generally it is less expensive in time, effort, and money to locate mediated learning materials commercially produced; however, many times commercial materials are unavailable or unsuitable to specific instructional applications. Locally produced learning materials can be more effective than commercially produced materials because of their up-to-date nature, their specific relationship to needs of the learner, and the positive correlation with the total course for which they were developed (19). In this respect, local production will be limited only by the technical capabilities of the LRC and staff and the imagination of instructors developing such materials.

Evaluation of production services, performance, and successful knowledge of up-dating instructional needs, requires continual input from instructors using the service and rationale from those not using the services. Production services effectiveness can not be based on the statistical analysis of productions completed, and materials circulated although this is a part of the information needed. Many other functions may yield other needed information on the success of production services but direct client evaluation will give the clearest picture from which inferences may be made regarding the efficiency and effectiveness of all functions either direct or indirect (26).

Three levels of local educational media production have been identified: mechanical, creative, and design (25, p. 9). Of these three the design level is the most important for it is here that the instructor analyzes instructional problems and the objectives of the production. Behaviorial changes are identified and achievement levels determined. Environmental conditions are assessed and message characteristics defined. The creative level requires the interpretation of decisions made during the design level into visual and audio elements. Mechanical elements are then concerned with the actual technical aspects of converting the design and creative elements into film, tape, or other forms of mediated instructional materials.

As an additional service, many LRC programs include production facilities, materials, equipment and instruction for student production work. Such services give students an alternative for developing information in non-traditional ways for class assignments and becomes an additional avenue for learning.

Distribution

The effective distribution of media and hardware becomes a problem on many campuses. Constraints contributing to the problem range from physical characteristics of the campus to a lack of awareness of materials and services available by faculty members. The stimulation of the use of hardware and software in a distribution program to meet potential or desirable volumes may become a critical problem for the LRC staff. Maximum use of materials should be the objective of any distribution program. This must be accomplished by developing a system which effectively and efficiently gets needed material to the instructor where it is wanted, when it is wanted, and the way it is wanted, and then ensures its return to the LRC with the least amount of effort on the part of the instructor.

YES, I CAN PRODUCE A MULTI-MEDIA SHOW ON QUADRATIC EQUATIONS, SHALL I SIGN SOPHIA ?

Physical and time constraints may dictate that the distribution program include remote facilities for hardware needed at locations far removed from the centralized distribution point. These remote facilities will be dictated by distances, access availability to presentation areas, and the availability of delivery personnel, vans, elevators, and time limitations.

Basic to effectively operated distribtuion and utilization programs is the centralization of all hardware and equipment purchases in the LRC staff. Existing hardware inventories and recommendations for future purchases must be centralized within the responsibility of the LRC. Success of hardware distribution systems appear to be dependent upon the LRC having access to instructional hardware and control over future hardware purchases. Benefits from this arrangement include access by all departments to all hardware owned, reduction of overall hardware purchasing, wiser hardware selection based on need, and a controlled maintenance and repair program (17).

An effective distribution system must address itself to what provision has been made to allow ease and convenience of the use of audiovisual hardware. Optimum results can be obtained only if proper architectural considerations have been made in conjunction with furnishings and hardware. Utilization will directly relate to the ease and speed with which audiovisual software can be used by instructors. Any major environmental adjustment that must be made will minimize the utilization of any form of media (37, p. 16-17).

Scheduling becomes a critical focal point in any distribution program. The scheduling process is the first point at which LRC staff comes into contact with users of its distribution services. The speed and ease with which scheduling is accomplished will be the users first impression of the distribution process and may well establish a positive attitude which will result in good will for the whole LRC program.

Many LRC distribution services includes a further service to its users. Presentation services includes not only delivery and set up of software and hardware to prescribed locations, but also includes personnel for the operation of the hardware.

In continued efforts to maintain and improve proper service levels for distribution and presentation services, feedback must be received from instructors using these services. An evaluation instrument of brevity and simplicity should be devised to answer the following questions: Is communications with faculty in the handling of request effective? Is the LRC staff treating the faculty with courtesy and respect? Is the equipment in proper working order and is the set up satisfactory? Does the faculty member have any recommendations to improve the services? Evaluation must be done on a day to day basis with responses to negative replies receiving immediate attention (30).

Maintenance and Repair

Any program using media software is highly dependent upon not only distribution services but the condition and operating efficiency of the hardware to be used. A strong program of maintenance, servicing, and repair is essential if the other services are to be satisfactory. Equipment care essentials should be carried out on a regular basis. Replacement equipment should be available in case of equipment breakdown and all repair work done as soon as possible so that down time for equipment is kept at a minimum. A hardware maintenance technician working from a centralized maintenance shop is needed for LRC programs of any size. In addition to regular maintenance and servicing schedules, regular preventive maintenance procedures for the periodic overhaul of equipment by their manufacturers should be planned. Standardization of hardware used makes upkeep and care far easier and results in fewer operator caused problems (15, pp. 328-39).

Systematic record keeping procedures for media hardware will provide information on the dependability of different makes and types of equipment, relative costs of repair and maintenance frequency of required replacement, adjustment, or repair, and the volume of maintenance work conducted during any particular period of time. Proper maintenance of media hardware is essential; without it, the quality of the LRC program will be reduced by inefficient performance (8, pp. 246-47).

Conclusions

The qualitative guidelines established by ALA, AACJC, and

I WANT TO CHECK OUT THESE BOOKS, AND PICK UP MY ILLUSTRATIONS, AND CHECK OUT SOME TAPES AND RENEW MY PICASSO, MAYBE I COULD RENT A DOLLY?
CARD

AECT have advanced the LRC concept from a program approach and not from quantitative standards or facilities. They provide a pattern in terms of structure, application to institutional planning, and variation in institutional objectives. Maximum flexibility has been provided leading to a coordination impossible to provide by a segmented organization of such services (40, pp. 219-33).

Today's higher education is unique in that its instruction depends greatly upon different approaches and technological elements. The provision of library and instructional materials goes far beyond traditional library and A-V department services. With students diverse and often less well prepared, instructional methods must be stressed to a far greater degree in higher education. Emphasis upon innovation in curricula and techniques of instruction are characteristics of LRC responses to these problems. Comprehensive education depends very heavily upon the materials, services, and technology of a properly administered Learning Resources Center (32).

CHAPTER BIBLIOGRAPHY

[1] AASL, ALA, and AECT, Media Programs: District and School, ALA and AECT, 1975.

[2] ALA, Library of Congress, Library Association, and the Canadian Library Association, Anglo-American Cataloging Rules, ALA, 1970.

[3] ACRL, AACJ and AECT, "Guidelines for Two-Year College Learning Resources Programs," Audiovisual Instruction, 18 (January 1973):50-61.

[4] ALA and NEA, Standards for School Media Programs, ALA and NEA, 1969.

[5] AECT, Planning and Operating Media Centers, AECT, 1975.

[6] AECT, Standards for Cataloging Nonprint Materials, 3d ed., AECT, 1972.

[7] Allen, Kenneth, and Allen, Loren, Organization and Administration of the Learning Resources Center in the Community College, Linnet Books, 1973.

[8] Brown, James W., ed., Educational Media Yearbook, 1974, Bowker, 1974.

[9] _____, Educational Media Yearbook, 1975-76, Bowker, 1975.

[10] Brown, James W.; Norberg, Kenneth D.; and Srygley, Sara K., Administering Educational Media: Instructional Technology and Library Services, McGraw-Hill, 1972.

[11] Carter, Mary Duncan; Bonk, Wallace John; and Magrill, Rose Mary, Building Library Collections, 4th ed., Scarecrow Press, Inc., 1974.

[12] Dallas Public Library, Nonbook Materials Policy/Procedure Manual, Prepared by the Nonbook Materials Task Force of the Dallas Public Library, 1974.

[13] Davis, Harold S., Instructional Media Center: Bold New Venture, Indiana University Press, 1971.

[14] Ducote, Richard, "The Learning Resources Center: Concepts and Designs," Boone, North Carolina, Appalachian State University, 1970.

[15] Erickson, Carlton, W. H., Administering Instructional Media Programs, Macmillan, 1969.

[16] Frederick, Frantz J., "Overview of Current Learning Theories for Media Centers," Library Trends 9 (April 1971):401-9.

[17] Gallup, David, and Griffin, Robert E., "Establishing and Administering an Effective Instructional Hardware Distribution Program," Audiovisual Instruction 20 (October 1975):16-20.

[18] Griffith, Alice B., "Building the Quality Book Collection," Junior College Journal 40 (June-July 1970):16-20.

[19] Grimes, George H., "Local Production and the Development Process," Audiovisual Instruction (November 1973).

[20] Grove, Pearce S., and Clement, Evelyn G., Bibliographic Control of Nonprint Media, Chicago, ALA, 1972.

[21] Hicks, Warren B., and Tillin, Alma M., Developing Multi-Media Libraries, Bowker, 1970.

[22] Hostrop, Richard W., Education Inside the Library-Media Center, Linnet Books, 1973.

[23] Johnson, Jean Thornton, et al., AV Cataloging and Processing Simplified, Raleigh, North Carolina, Audiovisual Catalogers, Inc., 1971.

[24] Johnson, Scottie McIntyre; Schexnaydre, Linda; and Woods, Mary S., Planning Audiovisual Services in Public Libraries, Austin, Texas State Library, 1975.

[25] Kemp, Jerrold E., Planning and Producing Audiovisual Materials, rev. ed., Chandler Publishing Co., 1968.

[26] Leonard, W. Patrick, and Warren, Sandra J., "Media Services Client Satisfaction as a Barometer," Audiovisual Instruction (September 1974):5-6.

[27] Lewis, Philip, "Introduction," Library Trends 19 (April 1971): 399-400.

[28] Limbacher, James L., A Reference Guide to Audiovisual Information, Bowker, 1972.

[29] Lyle, Guy R., The President, the Professor and the College Library, New York, Wilson, 1963.

[30] McCoy, David, "Continuous Evaluation of Instructional Media Services at Eastfield College," Audiovisual Instruction (September 1974):10-13.

[31] Mowery, Robert L., "The Trend to LC in Colleges and University Libraries," Library Resources and Technical Services 19 (Fall 1975):389-97.

[32] Pesking, Ira J., "The Junior College Library," Library Trends 23 (January 1975):383-90.

[33] Peterson, Gary T., "Conceptualizing the Learning Center," Audiovisual Instruction 18 (March 1973):67.

[34] Pearson, Neville, and Butler, Lucius A., eds., Learning Resource Centers, Burgess, 1973.

[35] _____, Instructional Materials Centers, Burgess, 1969.

[36] Postlethwait, S. N.; Novak, J.; and Murray, H. T., The Audio-Tutorial Approach to Learning, 2d ed., Burgess, 1969.

[37] Randall, Warren, "School Facilities Checklist," Audiovisual Instruction (December 1973):16-17.

[38] Rowell, John, and Heidbreder, M. Ann, Educational Media Selection Centers, ALA, 1971.

[39] U.S. Office of Education, Educational Technology: A Handbook of Standard Terminology and a Guide for Recording and Reporting Information About Educational Technology, National Center for Educational Statistics, U.S. Office of Education, 1974.

[40] Wallace, James O., "Two-Year College Library Standards," Library Trends, 21 (October 1972):219:33.

CHAPTER VIII

ESSENTIALS FOR AN EFFECTIVE LEARNING ENVIRONMENT

Aubrey D. Sharpe

Introduction

The task of a learning resource center or instructional media center is the facilitation of learning with respect to learning spaces, learning resources and instructional design (1, January 26, 1976). The scope of this chapter is learning spaces. The purpose is to examine some of the facilities of the community college that most directly affect instruction and learning, i.e., the classroom.

This study rests upon some basic assumptions about the learner, the instructor, the facilities and the media.

1. The learner is the center of the educative process. All other aspects of the process are evaluated on the basis of how they facilitate learning.

2. The instructor is the content specialist and learning leader or guide. This is the person to consult regarding the learning environment.

3. The facilities, in large measure, will determine the degree to which media will be used innovatively.

4. Media and curriculum are inseparable.

With these assumptions in mind, this study will use as its vehicle the model on the following page.

After examining these "essentials," the study will be concluded with some principles and suggestions concerning the planning of an effective learning environment.

Essential Considerations for
Classroom Facilities

Light and Light Control

The classroom environment should be characterized by a light control system which reflects the insight that various instructional tasks require varying amounts of illumination. Therefore, the viewing conditions within the classroom should be checked in terms of the kinds of observations pupils make and respond to during their learning activities. For example, the room needs to be darkened for picture projection and brightened for reading laboratory and other observations. This is the concept of "light control" (2, p. 110).

Whatever the design of the building, one should allow for and install light control facilities at the time of construction, for it is most difficult to have installation made afterwards (3, p. 78). Classrooms that feature solid walls of glass may present difficulties. Natural light is important, but it can be and should be controlled. In no case should a west wall contain large window areas, since heat buildup and light control may pose problems. Skylights should not be included in a classroom. They make the use of instructional media more difficult and may lead to major heating problems (4, pp. 36-37).

For classrooms with windows, there are three devices for light control widely used today. First, there are opaque drapes made of plastic flame-resistant material which do a fine job of controlling light. Secondly, there are plastic shades which must have light arresters around the edges and require closing of the windows. These are not recommended for large walls of windows. Third, there are full-closure venetian blinds. This method is highly popular and an effective means of light control in many classrooms (3, p. 78). There is no reason why a classroom cannot have both windows and media programs, but careful planning is required (4, p. 37).

The windowless classroom with artificial lighting and climate control more readily lends itself to effective light control.

Adequate Ventilation

Ventilation and light control should be considered together because one implicates the other. For example, a windowless classroom would require artificial lighting and climate control, but not shades, drapes or blinds.

Ventilating ducts should be placed so as not to interfere with the mounting of projection screws and so that display areas and chalkboards may be arranged appropriately at eye level. All who are concerned with effective instruction must call for the best decision possible regarding the ventilation problem in the classroom. Whatever the system, its adequacy must be emphasized during periods when drapes or other light control devices are in use. There seems to be agreement that a good standard for air exchange is fifteen cubic feet of air per minute for each student with proper room temperatures and humidity being maintained continuously. If drape systems are used in connection with window ventilating systems, they should be hung from the ceiling approximately eighteen inches from the window to permit at least a limited flow of incoming air (5, pp. 252-53). According to Evans and Neagley,

> Research indicates that students learn best when the conditions of the air and surrounding surfaces are most conducive to physical and mental well being. Although it is possible for the human organism to adjust itself to a wide variety of environmental conditions, it is done with a considerable expenditure of energy, which distracts the student from learning in an uncomfortable environment. Factors that must be considered in this respect are air temperature, radiant temperature, relative humidity, air motion, odors, dust and dirt, and atmospheric contaminants. (6, p. 208)

Evans and Neagley further say that "Because Community College buildings are used around the clock and during all seasons, total climate control is an absolute necessity . . . this is not the place to cut corners financially" (6, p. 208).

Acoustical Treatment

The increased use of audio-visual media and student activities in today's modern classroom as a result of our modern curriculum requires that the classroom be acoustically treated. Noise level for today's classroom should be no greater than 30-40 decibels at any given time (3, p. 79).

Therefore, in an effort to improve general learning conditions, and to improve the intelligibility of reproduced sounds, consideration ought to be given to acoustical treatment. At least ceilings should be acoustically treated to subdue the noise of regular classroom activities, which in the modern program include multi-group action. Acoustic planning of the entire building is important also to control the transmission of noise from corridor to classrooms and from gymnasiums and band rehearsal rooms to other nearby learning areas (5, p. 254).

In the Community College learning takes place through both traditional and innovative activities. In all of these activities the sound factor is of utmost importance. Undesirable and conflicting sounds hinder verbal communication between instructor and student and between student and student. In order to learn, students must not only hear distinctly, but they should be protected from distracting and nerve-jangling extraneous sounds (6, p. 209).

Acoustical treatment "deadens reverberations and permits speaking and listening comfort" (7, p. 24). This may be done by using "as many sound absorbing materials in construction as possible. Cork on walls, carpet on floors and drapes on windows are just a few ways to contain sound" (8, p. 20). Also, "Surrounding the instructor by hard surfaces, designing the ceiling to reflect sound to the audience, and covering rear walls with absorptive material are means of improving the acoustical quality of a larger room" (9, p. 66).

Electrical and Electronic Outlets

Education has only begun to use electronic teaching-learning equipment in its facilities. However, this use is sure to increase with the continuing development of technology for educational purposes. With overhead projectors commonplace, closed circuit televisions moving into the classroom and computer assisted instruction gaining momentum in the Community College, the electronic capability of the classroom is becoming even more important.

School building planners should see to it that as much oversized conduit and electrical wiring as possible are built into all new college buildings. Several outlets should be placed on each wall. "It would be wise to plan and place a number of electrical outlets in the floor of the room, approximately in the middle from side to side and at ten-foot intervals, running from the front of the room to the back. Brass plates, placed flush with the floor, are available for covering such outlets" (4, p. 37). These outlets should not be on the same circuit as the overhead lights, should deliver 110-130 volts, and be found for no less than 20 amps. Outlets and circuits should be arranged in such a way that several pieces of equipment may be used at the same time without overloading the circuit (3, p. 80).

Present and future instructional demands should be considered in providing adequate wiring (5, p. 339). For example, if instructional television is not presently being used, but could be used in the future, ducts for coaxial cable should be provided to allow for future flexibility and innovations (9, p. 69). Further, the building design should have empty conduits in walls, floors and ceilings so that T.V. cables and other wiring can be snaked through at a later date. Consideration should be given concerning where a T.V. set is going to be placed in the room before a decision to locate the antenna and closed-circuit outlets is made (8, p. 20).

Projection Facilities

Screens.--This is a very technical and important area of mediated instruction. Only a few guiding principles can be given here, however.

Not just any kind of screen will do. Screens should be selected appropriately in terms of the kind of material to be projected upon them, the size and shape of the classroom and placed properly for optimum viewing (5, p. 240).

There are many types of screens available. The following descriptions are of three of the more popular choices today:

Glass Beaded Screens are screens with surfaces covered with tiny glass beads which have the ability to reflect and refract light in such a way that a large percentage of the light is reflected back in the direction of the projector. The beaded screen reflects more light than the white matte within a seating area of about 22 degrees. However, the picture brightness falls off sharply as the viewing angle is increased.

White Matte Screens are smooth white surfaces reflecting less light than the beaded; however, the viewing angle is much greater: therefore, the white matte is recommended for use in square classrooms. Also, the matte surface screen is much more durable than the beaded surface.

Lenticular Screens are of highly reflective durable type surface with a wide viewing angle. There are two types of lenticular screens--one for a well-darkened classroom and one for use in classrooms which cannot be well darkened. This screen costs more than the other two discussed here (3, p. 79).

An important area of concern is screen image. Obviously, if a student is to see an image adequately, he cannot be seated too far away, too close to the screen, or too far to the side. The more students placed within this fan-shaped area, the more who will be able to gain maximum benefit from the presentation taking place. A corner screen location provides the best seating arrangement and insures the most efficient use of space. For good viewing there should be some light in the room. This permits students to take notes and to interact with the instructor (9, p. 66).

The bottom of the screen should be about eye level of the seated viewers. It is recommended that a square screen be used because of the various shapes of material to be projected. To determine the proper size screen for a given classroom, one should take one-sixth the length of the classroom (projection throw) and this will be the proper width of the screen needed for best viewing ease.

Projection.--Every classroom should have a projection stand as permanent equipment. This should be about 42 inches high with two or three shelves measuring 18 x 24 inches with 4 inch rubber wheels. Thus, the projection stand is mobile, adaptable, and may be used to hold projectors, record players, tape recorders, books and many other items commonly found in a classroom (3, p. 79).

A special low projection stand or other facility should be available for placement in front of the room by the instructor's station to accommodate the overhead projector. This low stand should have large rubber-tired wheels and may be used to accommodate the opaque projector.

In those rooms used most frequently for film projection, a small projection closet might prove useful. A closet in the rear of the room with a window at the height of a projector on a rolling cart cuts down projector noise and eliminates the nuisance of having to haul the projector in from another room; films are projected from the storage closet. The closet should also include speaker jacks for built-in ceiling speakers and storage shelves for films and other materials (8, p. 20).

Another innovation worth considering is the lectern control panel. A teacher's control panel should be provided on the lectern for control of lights and projection equipment during mediated presentations. The lectern may be movable and should be located out of the line of projection. Equipment controlled from the lectern might be: (1) room lights; (2) CCTV camera; (3) screen; (4) pointer, electric flashlight outlet; (5) overhead projector; (6) 16mm sound movie projector, automatic (off-on-advance-reverse); (7) 35mm filmstrip projector (off-on-advance-reverse); (8) microphone, with amplifier control to speakers and distribution to canels; (9) lectern speaker and headphone jack, to monitor canels; (10) speakers, microphone and monitor (10, p. 44).

Storage, Display and Work Areas*

(*Much of the material in this section was adapted from Media in Schools (3, pp. 79-80.)

In the era of the textbook-lecture centered curriculum, there was little need for storage, display and work areas other than the individual stations. However, our modern curriculum and teaching-learning methods and techniques require a great deal of flexible and adaptable storage, display and work area. Since many variables determine exactly what is needed in each situation, it is suggested that a flexible design be employed that can be readily modified to meet future needs and that the installations be multi-purpose.

The overriding consideration in planning facilities for effective use of instructional media is that the instructor should be able to obtain required material quickly. This suggests that audiovisual storage facilities might best be placed in the teaching areas as well as the resource center (9, p. 67). Storage space will be needed for such items as charts, maps, posters, films, filmstrips, slides, flat pictures and such A-V equipment as may be permanently placed in the classroom. Specifically needed are shelving for books and other materials; a cabinet with drawers of several sizes to accommodate materials and hand tools; large file cabinets; chart cabinets for charts up to 30 x 40 inches, posters, pictures and bulletin board materials which need to be laid flat.

The amount and type of display surfaces needed will be determined by the teaching-learning objectives of the curriculum. Therefore, consideration should be given to the installation of facilities which can easily be changed both verticle and horizontal display space and either increase or decrease the display area.

Chalkboards and bulletin boards should be placed at eye level of students, and should be well lighted. Light pastel colors for the surface of these items are highly desirable. Display areas may be increased by the installation of swinging bulletin boards with a number of leaves which may be turned at will. Pegboards equipped with hooks and other devices are becoming increasingly popular for display of three dimensional objects. A steel chalkboard may be used for a magnetic display.

Today's educational techniques require space for small group activities such as group discussions and project construction. These spaces should be adequate for both individual and group use. Locations should be provided where an individual or group can work with books, slides, filmstrips, film, videotape, or even interact with a computer via computer assisted instruction. In such locations, students should be able to take notes and use portable audiovisual equipment--under conditions affording acoustic and visual privacy (9, pp. 66-67).

Movable Furnishings

The modern classroom should be one of multiple use and

flexibility. The current curriculums at community colleges are emphasizing multiple teaching-learning activities and a great deal of student involvement. This new approach requires a classroom that can be adapted quickly and easily to most every teaching strategy and learning style.

"Don't bolt things down. Tables, chairs and other furnishings should be movable" (8, p. 21). If innovative, mediated instruction is to have maximum success, then this must be the motto in building and furnishing classrooms. The concept may be implemented by providing adequate storage space for items not in use; portable equipment and built-ins that are out of the way; collapsible and dual use shelving, chalkboards and display areas; work areas and cabinets on wheels; movable and accordian type walls; and as much dual use furniture as possible.

Principles for Planning an Effective Learning Environment

A General Statement

Classrooms should be designed and constructed in new ways. They should be built by persons of vision, who are willing to innovate, not only to meet today's problems and needs, but also to have a vision of the probable problems and needs of tomorrow.

The classroom of today should be somewhat larger than of yesterday (10); it should be flexible and adaptable; it should have adequate ventilation, proper light level at all work stations, up-to-date equipment, a basic library of instructional media and other media facilities for many and varied activities. A classroom of adequate size (1200 sq. feet as opposed to the traditional 700-900 squ. feet) and properly equipped should permit the application of the latest and most efficient means of programming and would allow students to progress under the guidance of the best equipped teacher, getting away from the old lecture-textbook method of instruction (3, p. 78).

Some Specific Principles

The following principles may prove beneficial to an administrator beginning to formulate his own philosophy of an effective learning environment. This is not a comprehensive list, but it does reflect the opinions of some experts in the field.

1. Planning of new or expanded facilities is accomplished with the participation and concurrence of the chief administrator in all details and with wide involvement of users and staff (12).

2. An educational media specialist should be consulted about specifications relative to media when plans are made for the construction of new buildings and the remodeling of old ones (11).

3. In order to avoid having to move classes to special rooms to make use of educational media, each classroom in all school buildings should be equipped with essential facilities for effective use of appropriate educational media; including telecasts, projected materials, recordings, and self-instruction devices (11).

4. Every classroom should be equipped with full light control, electrical outlets, forced ventilation, and educational media storage space (11).

5. Classrooms should be equipped with permanently installed bulletin boards, chalk boards, projection screens, map rails, and storage facilities needed for the particular type of instruction conducted in each room (11).

6. The physical facilities should provide a wide variety of learning and study situations (12).

7. The physical facilities should be attractive, comfortable and designed to encourage use by students (12).

8. The multimedia classroom is an attempt to improve the quality of instruction by making it convenient and attractive to both instructor and students to use several avenues of learning in a single class period (13, p. 95).

9. Faculty enthusiasm is the key to realization of the undoubted values of the improved instructional environment in the multimedia classroom. This enthusiasm seems connected to the

provision of release time to do necessary planning and proper training and assistance by competent technicians (13, p. 104).

Conclusion

The learning environment is an essential element in the development and transmission of an effective, innovative curriculum. The two should not be separated. The ingredients and principles concerning the learning environment discussed here are all aimed at making the educative experience as pleasurable as possible. Dr. Frank Brum, former educational advisor to President Johnson, says: "Classrooms must be carefully remodeled for comfort and pleasantness. The concept of a learning laboratory instead of a classroom for reluctant learners . . ." (7, p. 24) is what he seems to prefer. Robert Mager says it this way: "Things that are surrounded by unpleasantness are seldom surrounded by people" (14).

CHAPTER BIBLIOGRAPHY

[1] Miller, Bob W., Administration of Learning Resources in Higher Education, Class Notes (NTSU EDHE690), Spring 1976.

[2] Erickson, Carlton W. H., Fundamentals of Teaching with Audiovisual Technology, New York, The Macmillan Company, 1965.

[3] Farrar, W. W., ed., Media in Schools: A Handbook for Teachers and Administrators, Austin, Texas, Audio-Visual Education Association, November, 1967.

[4] Tanzman, John and Dunn, Kenneth, Using Instructional Media Effectively, New York, Parker Publishing Company, Inc., 1971.

[5] Erickson, Carlton W. H., Administering Audio-visual Services, New York, The Macmillan Company, 1959.

[6] Evans, N. Dean and Neagley, Ross L., Planning and Developing Innovative Community Colleges, Englewood Cliffs, Prentice Hall, Inc., 1973.

[7] Wittich, Walter A. and Schuller, Charles F. Audio-visual Materials: Their Nature and Use, New York, Harper & Row Publishers, 1967.

[8] Linton, Dolores and David, Practical Guide to Classroom Media, Dayton, Pflaum/Standard Publishing, 1971.

[9] Culclasure, David F., Effective Use of Audiovisual Media, Englewood Clitfs, Prentice-Hall, 1969.

[10] Instructional Hardware--A Guide to Architectural Requirements, New York, Educational Facilities Laboratories, 1970.

[11] Fulton, W. R., Criteria Relating to Educational Media Programs in School Systems, Norman, University of Oklahoma, n.d.

[12] Guidelines for Two-Year College Learning Resource Programs, American Library Association, American Association of Community and Junior Colleges and Association for Educational Communications and Technology, 1972.

[13] Thornton, James W. and Brown, James W. New Media and College Teaching, Washington, D.C., The Department of Audiovisual Instruction, N.E.A., 1968.

[14] Mager, Robert F. Developing an Attitude Toward Learning, Belmont, Fearon Publishers, 1968.

APPENDIX

DALLAS COUNTY COMMUNITY COLLEGE DISTRICT
LEARNING RESOURCES CENTER
MATERIALS SELECTION POLICY

PHILOSOPHY OF SELECTION

All materials acquired by the Learning Resources Centers should reflect resource needs of the Dallas County Community College District. This underlying principle will determine such basic matters as type, quantity and scope of resources to be acquired. In general, the resource needs of the Colleges should reflect one or more of the following:

(1) curriculum support
(2) general information
(3) general or special professional growth
(4) cultural enrichment
(5) extra curricular interests

RESPONSIBILITY FOR SELECTION

The responsibility for selection is vested in the staff of the Learning Resources Center, which has the obligation of working closely with both faculty and students in coordinating the selection of materials and helping to build a collection that truly reflects resource needs of the Colleges.

CONTROL OF RESOURCES

The Learning Resources Center will retain control of all resources purchased through its budget and/or placed on its inventory.

PRINCIPLES OF RESOURCES SELECTION

The Learning Resources Center is committed to the principles supported by the American Library Association's Library Bill of Rights in that it must provide:

(1) materials that will enrich and support the curriculum, taking into consideration the varied interests, abilities and maturity levels of the users served.

(2) materials that will stimulate growth in factual knowledge, literacy appreciation, aesthetic values, and ethical standards
(3) materials that supply a background of information which will enable users to make intelligent judgments in their daily lives
(4) materials on opposing side of controversial issues, so that students may develop under guidance the practice of critical reading and thinking
(5) materials representative of the many religious, ethnic and cultural groups and their contributions to the American heritage
(6) materials on various learning and interest levels necessary to compliment the open door policy of the community college

Print materials that meet one or more of the following evaluative criteria may be considered for inclusion in the collection:

(1) importance of subject matter to curriculum
(2) permanent or timely value
(3) competent and qualified author, editor or compiler
(4) accuracy of information
(5) readability
(6) reputation and professional standing of publisher
(7) price
(8) format
(9) availability of material elsewhere in community
(10) scarcity of material available
(11) interest by student or faculty
(12) historical value

Serial publications that meet such of the following criteria as are applicable may be considered for inclusion in the collection:

(1) importance of title to the curriculum
(2) scarcity of materials in other formats
(3) indexing in standard indexes
(4) presentation on the community college students' reading and interest level
(5) availability of back issues on microfilm
(6) number of journals received in the subject area
(7) price

Non-print materials that meet one or more of the following evaluative criteria may be considered for inclusion in the collection:

(1) enrichment and support to curriculum
(2) appropriateness for age, intelligence, abilities and interest of students
(3) technical and artistic quality
(4) authority of producer
(5) contribution of uniqueness or significance by the presentation or content
(6) price
(7) availability of material in other formats
(8) scarcity of material available
(9) interest by student or faculty

Systematic withdrawals will be conducted of out-dated, damaged and worn materials no longer useful.

Gifts must meet the same criteria as new materials to be included in the library's collection. Acceptance of a gift does not imply in lusion in the collection; the LRC must be free to dispose of gifts as it sees fit. No value appraisals will be written.

The request of any individual or group to withdraw any materials from the Learning Resource Center's collection shall be referred to the appropriate staff member as outlined in each campuses re-examination of materials procedure.

PROCEDURES FOR HANDLING QUESTIONED MATERIALS

1. When a complaint is received, the patron is referred to the appropriate Director (Library or Media). If this person is not available, the librarian/media specialist who received the complaint may meet with the patron if it is possible. Should skeleton staffing or other problems prevent the professional from meeting with the patron, the patron's name, phone number and mailing address are taken so arrangements can be made for a meeting at the earliest possible date.

2. The appropriate person or persons are informed of the complaint as soon as possible.

3. The librarian/media specialist meeting with the patron inquires about the nature of the complaint, allowing the patron to speak freely without interruption.

4. The librarian/media specialist discusses the objections with the patron explaining the basic philosophy contained in the materials selection policy.

5. The librarian/media specialist asks the patron for recommendations regarding the material referring to the LRC policy and procedure in this situation.

6. If the patron is not satisfied with the explanation given, the librarian/media specialist will give the patron a copy of the Patron Objection to Materials Form to be completed. The patron may take the form home and return it by mail.

7. No commitment should be made by the librarian/media specialist at this time.

8. It is important that the patron leave the library feeling that the complaint has been received courteously and in a responsible manner.

9. The appropriate person or persons is informed of the follow-up meeting.

10. When the complaint form is returned, it is turned over to the Assistant Dean of Learning Resources, along with any reviews, explanations, etc. by the librarian/media specialist.

11. The Assistant Dean of Learning Resources then informs the Dean of Instruction who calls an ad hoc committee comprised of: Dean of Instruction, Assistant Dean of Learning Resources, appropriate Director (Library or Media) and two faculty members from the most appropriate divisions.

12. This committee will review the complaint in consideration with the basic philosophy contained in the materials selection policy and the DCCCD philosophy.

13. The committee's decision will be in the form of a written letter to the patron.

DALLAS COUNTY COMMUNITY COLLEGE DISTRICT

Patron Objection to LRC Materials

Please complete the following concerning the material in question and return to:

Format (book, record, film, tape, etc.)_____
Author:_____
Title:_____
Producer or Publisher:_____
Patron's Name:_____
Telephone:_____Address:_____
City:_____Zip Code:_____

1. Do you represent an organization?____If so, please identify it.
2. Have you read, seen or heard this material in its entirety? ____If not, which parts?_____
3. To what in this material did you object? (Please be specific: if printed material, cite page)_____
4. Do you believe there is anything good about this material?___
5. Do you think faculty would use this material?_____
6. Are you familiar with reviews of this material?_____
7. Can you recommend better material of this kind?_____

_____   _____
(date)   (patron's signature)

Note to patron: Your concern is appreciated. Your objection will be referred to the appropriate committee. You will receive a written response concerning their decision as soon as possible.